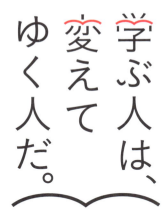

学ぶ人は、
変えて
ゆく人だ。

目の前にある問題はもちろん、
人生の問いや、
社会の課題を自ら見つけ、
挑み続けるために、人は学ぶ。
「学び」で、
少しずつ世界は変えてゆける。
いつでも、どこでも、誰でも、
学ぶことができる世の中へ。

旺文社

JN249193

2023年度版

※ 英検®には複数の方式があります（p.11参照）。本書に収録されている問題は、「従来型」の過去問のうち、公益財団法人 日本英語検定協会から提供を受けたもののみです。準会場・海外受験などの問題とは一致しない場合があります。英検S-CBTの過去問は公表されていませんが、問題形式・内容は従来型と変わりませんので、受験準備のためには本書収録の過去問がご利用いただけます。

※ このコンテンツは、公益財団法人 日本英語検定協会の承認や推奨、その他の検討を受けたものではありません。

英検®は、公益財団法人 日本英語検定協会の登録商標です。　旺文社

A Shortage of Doctors

Nowadays, some parts of Japan do not have enough doctors. It is said that many doctors prefer to work in cities, and this can cause problems for people living in rural areas. A shortage of doctors will prevent these people from receiving good medical treatment, so it is a serious issue. Many people say the government needs to do more about this situation.

Your story should begin with this sentence: **One day, Mr. and Mrs. Kato were talking about going to the beach.**

Promoting New Products

Today, some high-quality products are very expensive, so many people worry about whether they should buy them or not. Now, systems that allow people to rent a variety of products monthly are attracting attention. Some companies offer such systems, and by doing so they let people try items before buying them. With such systems, companies can promote their products more effectively.

Your story should begin with this sentence: **One evening, Mr. and Mrs. Kimura were talking about renting a car and going camping by a lake.**

Learning about Food

These days, many people are paying more attention to food safety. Because of this, food companies around Japan are trying to let customers know more about their products. Many of these companies use their websites to provide information about how food is produced. Customers check such information, and by doing so they learn more about the food products they purchase.

Your story should begin with this sentence: **One day, Miki was talking to her father in the kitchen.**

Protecting Important Sites

Nowadays, more places are being listed as World Heritage sites. However, many natural disasters are happening around the world. Some World Heritage sites have been seriously damaged by them, so they require a lot of work to repair. Communities need to work together to keep World Heritage sites in good condition. It is important to look after such sites for future generations.

Your story should begin with this sentence: **One day, Mr. and Mrs. Ito were talking about their trip.**

2021年度 第3回 二次試験 A日程 (2022.2.20 実施)

問題カード

この問題カードは切り取って、本番の面接の練習用にしてください。
質問は p.91 にありますので、参考にしてください。

Healthy Workers

A lot of people in Japan get a medical checkup every year. Some organizations offer a useful service for this. These organizations send special buses that provide medical checkups at the workplace. Many companies use such buses, and by doing so they help busy workers to stay healthy. It is very important that people try to get a medical checkup regularly.

Your story should begin with this sentence: **One morning, Mr. and Mrs. Mori were talking in their living room.**

Unusual Sea Life

These days, scientists are interested in knowing more about creatures that live deep in the world's oceans. However, reaching areas that are deep in the ocean is very dangerous. Now, some scientists send robots to such areas, and by doing so they can learn about unusual sea life safely. These robots will probably become more and more useful in the future.

Your story should begin with this sentence: **One day, Ken and his mother were talking in their living room.**

2022年度第2回　英検2級　解答用紙

【注意事項】
① 解答にはHBの黒鉛筆（シャープペンシルも可）を使用し，解答を訂正する場合には消しゴムで完全に消してください。
② 解答用紙は絶対に汚したり折り曲げたり，所定以外のところへの記入はしないでください。
③ マーク例　良い例 ● 　悪い例

これ以下の濃さのマークは読めません。

解答欄　1

問題番号	1	2	3	4
(1)	①	②	③	④
(2)	①	②	③	④
(3)	①	②	③	④
(4)	①	②	③	④
(5)	①	②	③	④
(6)	①	②	③	④
(7)	①	②	③	④
(8)	①	②	③	④
(9)	①	②	③	④
(10)	①	②	③	④
(11)	①	②	③	④
(12)	①	②	③	④
(13)	①	②	③	④
(14)	①	②	③	④
(15)	①	②	③	④
(16)	①	②	③	④
(17)	①	②	③	④
(18)	①	②	③	④
(19)	①	②	③	④
(20)	①	②	③	④

解答欄　2

問題番号	1	2	3	4
(21)	①	②	③	④
(22)	①	②	③	④
(23)	①	②	③	④
(24)	①	②	③	④
(25)	①	②	③	④
(26)	①	②	③	④

解答欄　3

問題番号	1	2	3	4
(27)	①	②	③	④
(28)	①	②	③	④
(29)	①	②	③	④
(30)	①	②	③	④
(31)	①	②	③	④
(32)	①	②	③	④
(33)	①	②	③	④
(34)	①	②	③	④
(35)	①	②	③	④
(36)	①	②	③	④
(37)	①	②	③	④
(38)	①	②	③	④

※筆記4の解答欄はこの裏にあります。

リスニング解答欄

問題番号	1	2	3	4
No.1	①	②	③	④
No.2	①	②	③	④
No.3	①	②	③	④
No.4	①	②	③	④
No.5	①	②	③	④
No.6	①	②	③	④
No.7	①	②	③	④
No.8	①	②	③	④
No.9	①	②	③	④
No.10	①	②	③	④
No.11	①	②	③	④
No.12	①	②	③	④
No.13	①	②	③	④
No.14	①	②	③	④
No.15	①	②	③	④
No.16	①	②	③	④
No.17	①	②	③	④
No.18	①	②	③	④
No.19	①	②	③	④
No.20	①	②	③	④
No.21	①	②	③	④
No.22	①	②	③	④
No.23	①	②	③	④
No.24	①	②	③	④
No.25	①	②	③	④
No.26	①	②	③	④
No.27	①	②	③	④
No.28	①	②	③	④
No.29	①	②	③	④
No.30	①	②	③	④

第1部：No.1〜No.15
第2部：No.16〜No.30

2022年度第2回
Web特典「自動採点サービス」対応 オンラインマークシート

※検定の回によって2次元コードが違います。
※筆記1〜3，リスニングの採点ができます。
※PCからも利用できます（本書 p.8 参照）。

※実際の解答用紙に似せていますが，デザイン・サイズは異なります。

●記入上の注意（記述形式）
・指示事項を守り，文字は，はっきりと分かりやすく書いてください。
・太枠に囲まれた部分のみが採点の対象です。

4 ライティング解答欄

2022年度第1回 英検2級 解答用紙

【注意事項】
① 解答にはHBの黒鉛筆(シャープペンシルも可)を使用し、解答を訂正する場合には消しゴムで完全に消してください。
② 解答用紙は絶対に汚したり折り曲げたり、所定以外のところへの記入はしないでください。

③ マーク例

良い例	悪い例
●	

これ以下の濃さのマークは読めません。

解答欄 1

問題番号	1	2	3	4
(1)	①	②	③	④
(2)	①	②	③	④
(3)	①	②	③	④
(4)	①	②	③	④
(5)	①	②	③	④
(6)	①	②	③	④
(7)	①	②	③	④
(8)	①	②	③	④
(9)	①	②	③	④
(10)	①	②	③	④
(11)	①	②	③	④
(12)	①	②	③	④
(13)	①	②	③	④
(14)	①	②	③	④
(15)	①	②	③	④
(16)	①	②	③	④
(17)	①	②	③	④
(18)	①	②	③	④
(19)	①	②	③	④
(20)	①	②	③	④

解答欄 2

問題番号	1	2	3	4
(21)	①	②	③	④
(22)	①	②	③	④
(23)	①	②	③	④
(24)	①	②	③	④
(25)	①	②	③	④
(26)	①	②	③	④

解答欄 3

問題番号	1	2	3	4
(27)	①	②	③	④
(28)	①	②	③	④
(29)	①	②	③	④
(30)	①	②	③	④
(31)	①	②	③	④
(32)	①	②	③	④
(33)	①	②	③	④
(34)	①	②	③	④
(35)	①	②	③	④
(36)	①	②	③	④
(37)	①	②	③	④
(38)	①	②	③	④

※筆記4の解答欄はこの裏にあります。

リスニング解答欄

問題番号	1	2	3	4
No.1	①	②	③	④
No.2	①	②	③	④
No.3	①	②	③	④
No.4	①	②	③	④
No.5	①	②	③	④
No.6	①	②	③	④
No.7	①	②	③	④
No.8	①	②	③	④
No.9	①	②	③	④
No.10	①	②	③	④
No.11	①	②	③	④
No.12	①	②	③	④
No.13	①	②	③	④
No.14	①	②	③	④
No.15	①	②	③	④
No.16	①	②	③	④
No.17	①	②	③	④
No.18	①	②	③	④
No.19	①	②	③	④
No.20	①	②	③	④
No.21	①	②	③	④
No.22	①	②	③	④
No.23	①	②	③	④
No.24	①	②	③	④
No.25	①	②	③	④
No.26	①	②	③	④
No.27	①	②	③	④
No.28	①	②	③	④
No.29	①	②	③	④
No.30	①	②	③	④

(第1部: No.1〜No.15 / 第2部: No.16〜No.30)

2022年度第1回

Web特典「自動採点サービス」対応 オンラインマークシート

※検定の回によって2次元コードが違います。
※筆記1〜3、リスニングの採点ができます。
※PCからも利用できます(本書p.8参照)。

※実際の解答用紙に似せていますが、デザイン・サイズは異なります。

切り取り線

●記入上の注意（記述形式）
・指示事項を守り，文字は，はっきりと分かりやすく書いてください。
・太枠に囲まれた部分のみが採点の対象です。

4 ライティング解答欄

5

10

15

2021年度第3回　英検2級　解答用紙

【注意事項】
①解答にはHBの黒鉛筆（シャープペンシルも可）を使用し，解答を訂正する場合には消しゴムで完全に消してください。
②解答用紙は絶対に汚したり折り曲げたり，所定以外のところへの記入はしないでください。

③マーク例

良い例	悪い例
●	

これ以下の濃さのマークは読めません。

解答欄 1

問題番号	1	2	3	4
(1)	①	②	③	④
(2)	①	②	③	④
(3)	①	②	③	④
(4)	①	②	③	④
(5)	①	②	③	④
(6)	①	②	③	④
(7)	①	②	③	④
(8)	①	②	③	④
(9)	①	②	③	④
(10)	①	②	③	④
(11)	①	②	③	④
(12)	①	②	③	④
(13)	①	②	③	④
(14)	①	②	③	④
(15)	①	②	③	④
(16)	①	②	③	④
(17)	①	②	③	④
(18)	①	②	③	④
(19)	①	②	③	④
(20)	①	②	③	④

解答欄 2

問題番号	1	2	3	4
(21)	①	②	③	④
(22)	①	②	③	④
(23)	①	②	③	④
(24)	①	②	③	④
(25)	①	②	③	④
(26)	①	②	③	④

解答欄 3

問題番号	1	2	3	4
(27)	①	②	③	④
(28)	①	②	③	④
(29)	①	②	③	④
(30)	①	②	③	④
(31)	①	②	③	④
(32)	①	②	③	④
(33)	①	②	③	④
(34)	①	②	③	④
(35)	①	②	③	④
(36)	①	②	③	④
(37)	①	②	③	④
(38)	①	②	③	④

※筆記4の解答欄はこの裏にあります。

リスニング解答欄

問題番号	1	2	3	4
No.1	①	②	③	④
No.2	①	②	③	④
No.3	①	②	③	④
No.4	①	②	③	④
No.5	①	②	③	④
No.6	①	②	③	④
No.7	①	②	③	④
No.8	①	②	③	④
No.9	①	②	③	④
No.10	①	②	③	④
No.11	①	②	③	④
No.12	①	②	③	④
No.13	①	②	③	④
No.14	①	②	③	④
No.15	①	②	③	④
No.16	①	②	③	④
No.17	①	②	③	④
No.18	①	②	③	④
No.19	①	②	③	④
No.20	①	②	③	④
No.21	①	②	③	④
No.22	①	②	③	④
No.23	①	②	③	④
No.24	①	②	③	④
No.25	①	②	③	④
No.26	①	②	③	④
No.27	①	②	③	④
No.28	①	②	③	④
No.29	①	②	③	④
No.30	①	②	③	④

第1部：No.1〜No.15
第2部：No.16〜No.30

2021年度第3回　Web特典「自動採点サービス」対応
オンラインマークシート
※検定の回によって2次元コードが違います。
※筆記1〜3，リスニングの採点ができます。
※PCからも利用できます（本書p.8参照）。

※実際の解答用紙に似せていますが，デザイン・サイズは異なります。

●記入上の注意（記述形式）
・指示事項を守り，文字は，はっきりと分かりやすく書いてください。
・太枠に囲まれた部分のみが採点の対象です。

4 ライティング解答欄

5

10

15

2021年度第2回　英検2級　解答用紙

【注意事項】
① 解答にはHBの黒鉛筆（シャープペンシルも可）を使用し，解答を訂正する場合には消しゴムで完全に消してください。
② 解答用紙は絶対に汚したり折り曲げたり，所定以外のところへの記入はしないでください。

③ マーク例

これ以下の濃さのマークは読めません。

解答欄 1

問題番号	1	2	3	4
(1)	①	②	③	④
(2)	①	②	③	④
(3)	①	②	③	④
(4)	①	②	③	④
(5)	①	②	③	④
(6)	①	②	③	④
(7)	①	②	③	④
(8)	①	②	③	④
(9)	①	②	③	④
(10)	①	②	③	④
(11)	①	②	③	④
(12)	①	②	③	④
(13)	①	②	③	④
(14)	①	②	③	④
(15)	①	②	③	④
(16)	①	②	③	④
(17)	①	②	③	④
(18)	①	②	③	④
(19)	①	②	③	④
(20)	①	②	③	④

解答欄 2

問題番号	1	2	3	4
(21)	①	②	③	④
(22)	①	②	③	④
(23)	①	②	③	④
(24)	①	②	③	④
(25)	①	②	③	④
(26)	①	②	③	④

解答欄 3

問題番号	1	2	3	4
(27)	①	②	③	④
(28)	①	②	③	④
(29)	①	②	③	④
(30)	①	②	③	④
(31)	①	②	③	④
(32)	①	②	③	④
(33)	①	②	③	④
(34)	①	②	③	④
(35)	①	②	③	④
(36)	①	②	③	④
(37)	①	②	③	④
(38)	①	②	③	④

※筆記4の解答欄はこの裏にあります。

リスニング解答欄

問題番号	1	2	3	4
No.1	①	②	③	④
No.2	①	②	③	④
No.3	①	②	③	④
No.4	①	②	③	④
No.5	①	②	③	④
No.6	①	②	③	④
No.7	①	②	③	④
No.8	①	②	③	④
No.9	①	②	③	④
No.10	①	②	③	④
No.11	①	②	③	④
No.12	①	②	③	④
No.13	①	②	③	④
No.14	①	②	③	④
No.15	①	②	③	④
No.16	①	②	③	④
No.17	①	②	③	④
No.18	①	②	③	④
No.19	①	②	③	④
No.20	①	②	③	④
No.21	①	②	③	④
No.22	①	②	③	④
No.23	①	②	③	④
No.24	①	②	③	④
No.25	①	②	③	④
No.26	①	②	③	④
No.27	①	②	③	④
No.28	①	②	③	④
No.29	①	②	③	④
No.30	①	②	③	④

第1部：No.1〜No.15
第2部：No.16〜No.30

2021年度第2回
Web特典「自動採点サービス」対応 オンラインマークシート

※検定の回によって2次元コードが違います。
※筆記1〜3，リスニングの採点ができます。
※PCからも利用できます（本書 p.8 参照）。

※実際の解答用紙に似せていますが，デザイン・サイズは異なります。

切り取り線

切り取り線

●記入上の注意（記述形式）
・指示事項を守り，文字は，はっきりと分かりやすく書いてください。
・太枠に囲まれた部分のみが採点の対象です。

4 ライティング解答欄

5
10
15

2021年度第1回　英検2級　解答用紙

【注意事項】
①解答にはHBの黒鉛筆（シャープペンシルも可）を使用し、解答を訂正する場合には消しゴムで完全に消してください。
②解答用紙は絶対に汚したり折り曲げたり、所定以外のところへの記入はしないでください。

③マーク例

良い例	悪い例
●	◐ ✗ ◖

これ以下の濃さのマークは読めません。

解答欄

問題番号	1	2	3	4
(1)	①	②	③	④
(2)	①	②	③	④
(3)	①	②	③	④
(4)	①	②	③	④
(5)	①	②	③	④
(6)	①	②	③	④
(7)	①	②	③	④
(8)	①	②	③	④
(9)	①	②	③	④
(10)	①	②	③	④
(11)	①	②	③	④
(12)	①	②	③	④
(13)	①	②	③	④
(14)	①	②	③	④
(15)	①	②	③	④
(16)	①	②	③	④
(17)	①	②	③	④
(18)	①	②	③	④
(19)	①	②	③	④
(20)	①	②	③	④

（1）

解答欄

問題番号	1	2	3	4
(21)	①	②	③	④
(22)	①	②	③	④
(23)	①	②	③	④
(24)	①	②	③	④
(25)	①	②	③	④
(26)	①	②	③	④

（2）

解答欄

問題番号	1	2	3	4
(27)	①	②	③	④
(28)	①	②	③	④
(29)	①	②	③	④
(30)	①	②	③	④
(31)	①	②	③	④
(32)	①	②	③	④
(33)	①	②	③	④
(34)	①	②	③	④
(35)	①	②	③	④
(36)	①	②	③	④
(37)	①	②	③	④
(38)	①	②	③	④

（3）

※筆記4の解答欄はこの裏にあります。

リスニング解答欄

問題番号	1	2	3	4
No.1	①	②	③	④
No.2	①	②	③	④
No.3	①	②	③	④
No.4	①	②	③	④
No.5	①	②	③	④
No.6	①	②	③	④
No.7	①	②	③	④
No.8	①	②	③	④
No.9	①	②	③	④
No.10	①	②	③	④
No.11	①	②	③	④
No.12	①	②	③	④
No.13	①	②	③	④
No.14	①	②	③	④
No.15	①	②	③	④
No.16	①	②	③	④
No.17	①	②	③	④
No.18	①	②	③	④
No.19	①	②	③	④
No.20	①	②	③	④
No.21	①	②	③	④
No.22	①	②	③	④
No.23	①	②	③	④
No.24	①	②	③	④
No.25	①	②	③	④
No.26	①	②	③	④
No.27	①	②	③	④
No.28	①	②	③	④
No.29	①	②	③	④
No.30	①	②	③	④

（第1部：No.1～No.15／第2部：No.16～No.30）

2021年度第1回

Web特典「自動採点サービス」対応オンラインマークシート
※検定の回によって2次元コードが違います。
※筆記1～3、リスニングの採点ができます。
※ PCからも利用できます（本書 p.8 参照）。

※実際の解答用紙に似せていますが、デザイン・サイズは異なります。

切り取り線

●記入上の注意（記述形式）
・指示事項を守り，文字は，はっきりと分かりやすく書いてください。
・太枠に囲まれた部分のみが採点の対象です。

4 ライティング解答欄

5
10
15

2020年度第3回　英検2級　解答用紙

【注意事項】
① 解答にはHBの黒鉛筆（シャープペンシルも可）を使用し，解答を訂正する場合には消しゴムで完全に消してください。
② 解答用紙は絶対に汚したり折り曲げたり，所定以外のところへの記入はしないでください。

③ マーク例

良い例	悪い例
●	

これ以下の濃さのマークは読めません。

解答欄 1

問題番号	1	2	3	4
(1)	①	②	③	④
(2)	①	②	③	④
(3)	①	②	③	④
(4)	①	②	③	④
(5)	①	②	③	④
(6)	①	②	③	④
(7)	①	②	③	④
(8)	①	②	③	④
(9)	①	②	③	④
(10)	①	②	③	④
(11)	①	②	③	④
(12)	①	②	③	④
(13)	①	②	③	④
(14)	①	②	③	④
(15)	①	②	③	④
(16)	①	②	③	④
(17)	①	②	③	④
(18)	①	②	③	④
(19)	①	②	③	④
(20)	①	②	③	④

解答欄 2

問題番号	1	2	3	4
(21)	①	②	③	④
(22)	①	②	③	④
(23)	①	②	③	④
(24)	①	②	③	④
(25)	①	②	③	④
(26)	①	②	③	④

解答欄 3

問題番号	1	2	3	4
(27)	①	②	③	④
(28)	①	②	③	④
(29)	①	②	③	④
(30)	①	②	③	④
(31)	①	②	③	④
(32)	①	②	③	④
(33)	①	②	③	④
(34)	①	②	③	④
(35)	①	②	③	④
(36)	①	②	③	④
(37)	①	②	③	④
(38)	①	②	③	④

※筆記4の解答欄はこの裏にあります。

リスニング解答欄

問題番号	1	2	3	4
No.1	①	②	③	④
No.2	①	②	③	④
No.3	①	②	③	④
No.4	①	②	③	④
No.5	①	②	③	④
No.6	①	②	③	④
No.7	①	②	③	④
No.8	①	②	③	④
No.9	①	②	③	④
No.10	①	②	③	④
No.11	①	②	③	④
No.12	①	②	③	④
No.13	①	②	③	④
No.14	①	②	③	④
No.15	①	②	③	④
No.16	①	②	③	④
No.17	①	②	③	④
No.18	①	②	③	④
No.19	①	②	③	④
No.20	①	②	③	④
No.21	①	②	③	④
No.22	①	②	③	④
No.23	①	②	③	④
No.24	①	②	③	④
No.25	①	②	③	④
No.26	①	②	③	④
No.27	①	②	③	④
No.28	①	②	③	④
No.29	①	②	③	④
No.30	①	②	③	④

第1部: No.1〜No.15
第2部: No.16〜No.30

2020年度第3回
Web特典「自動採点サービス」対応オンラインマークシート
※検定の回によって2次元コードが違います。
※筆記1〜3，リスニングの採点ができます。
※PCからも利用できます（本書 p.8 参照）。

※実際の解答用紙に似せていますが，デザイン・サイズは異なります。

切り取り線

●記入上の注意（記述形式）
・指示事項を守り，文字は，はっきりと分かりやすく書いてください。
・太枠に囲まれた部分のみが採点の対象です。

4 ライティング解答欄

	5
	10
	15

はじめに

実用英語技能検定（英検®）は，年間受験者数410万人（英検IBA，英検Jr. との総数）の小学生から社会人まで，幅広い層が受験する国内最大級の資格試験で，1963年の第1回検定からの累計では1億人を超える人々が受験しています。英検®は，コミュニケーションに欠かすことのできない4技能をバランスよく測定することを目的としており，英検®の受験によってご自身の英語力を把握できるだけでなく，進学・就職・留学などの場面で多くのチャンスを手に入れることにつながります。

この『全問題集シリーズ』は，英語を学ぶ皆さまを応援する気持ちを込めて刊行しました。本書は，2022年度第2回検定を含む6回分の過去問を，皆さまの理解が深まるよう，日本語訳や詳しい解説を加えて収録しています。また，正答率が高かった設問の解説には 正答率 ★75%以上 マーク（別冊p.2参照）がついているので，特におさえておきたい問題を簡単にチェックできます。

本書が皆さまの英検合格の足がかりとなり，さらには国際社会で活躍できるような生きた英語を身につけるきっかけとなることを願っています。

最後に，本書を刊行するにあたり，多大なご尽力をいただきました青山学院高等部 田辺博史先生に深く感謝の意を表します。

2023年　春

もくじ

Contents

本書の使い方 ……………………………………………… 3

音声について ……………………………………………… 4

Web特典について ………………………………………… 7

自動採点サービスの利用方法 …………………………… 8

英検インフォメーション ………………………………… 10
試験内容／英検の種類／合否判定方法／英検(従来型)受験情報─2023年度
試験日程・申込方法

2022年度の傾向と攻略ポイント ……………………… 14

二次試験・面接の流れ …………………………………… 16

2022年度	第2回検定（筆記・リスニング・面接） ····· 17
	第1回検定（筆記・リスニング・面接） ····· 43
2021年度	第3回検定（筆記・リスニング・面接） ····· 69
	第2回検定（筆記・リスニング・面接） ····· 95
	第1回検定（筆記・リスニング・面接） ··· 121
2020年度	第3回検定（筆記・リスニング・面接） ··· 147

執　　筆：田辺 博史（青山学院高等部）
編集協力：株式会社シー・レップス，鹿島 由紀子，久島 智津子，みけ みわ子
録　　音：ユニバ合同会社
デザイン：林 慎一郎（及川真咲デザイン事務所）
組版・データ作成協力：幸和印刷株式会社

本書の使い方

ここでは，本書の過去問および特典についての活用法の一例を紹介します。

本書の内容

- 過去問 6回分
- 英検インフォメーション (p.10-13)
- 2022年度の傾向と攻略ポイント (p.14-15)
- 二次試験・面接の流れ (p.16)
- Web特典 (p.7-9)

本書の使い方

一次試験対策

情報収集・傾向把握
・英検インフォメーション
・2022年度の傾向と攻略ポイント

過去問にチャレンジ
・2022年度第2回一次試験
・2022年度第1回一次試験
・2021年度第3回一次試験
・2021年度第2回一次試験
・2021年度第1回一次試験
・2020年度第3回一次試験
※【Web特典】自動採点サービスの活用

二次試験対策

情報収集・傾向把握
・二次試験・面接の流れ
・【Web特典】
　面接シミュレーション／面接模範例

過去問にチャレンジ
・2022年度第2回二次試験
・2022年度第1回二次試験
・2021年度第3回二次試験
・2021年度第2回二次試験
・2021年度第1回二次試験
・2020年度第3回二次試験

過去問の取り組み方

1セット目
【本番モード】
本番の試験と同じように，制限時間を設けて取り組みましょう。どの問題形式に時間がかかりすぎているか，正答率が低いかなど，今のあなたの実力を把握しましょう。
「自動採点サービス」を活用して，答え合わせをスムーズに行いましょう。

2〜5セット目
【学習モード】
制限時間をなくし，解けるまで取り組みましょう。
リスニングは音声を繰り返し聞いて解答を導き出してもかまいません。すべての問題に正解できるまで見直します。

6セット目
【仕上げモード】
試験直前の仕上げに利用しましょう。時間を計って本番のつもりで取り組みます。
これまでに取り組んだ6セットの過去問で間違えた問題の解説を本番試験の前にもう一度見直しましょう。

3

音声について

一次試験・リスニングと二次試験・面接の音声を聞くことができます。本書とともに使い，効果的なリスニング・面接対策をしましょう。

収録内容と特長

 一次試験・リスニング

本番の試験の音声を収録	➡	スピードをつかめる！
解答時間は本番通り10秒間	➡	解答時間に慣れる！
収録されている英文は，別冊解答に掲載	➡	聞き取れない箇所を確認できる！

 二次試験・面接（スピーキング）

| 実際の流れ通りに収録 | ➡ | 本番の雰囲気を味わえる！ |

・パッセージの黙読（試験通り20秒の黙読時間があります）
・パッセージの音読（Model Readingを収録しています）
・質問（音声を一時停止してご利用ください）

| 各質問のModel Answerも収録 | ➡ | 模範解答が確認できる！ |
| Model Answerは，別冊解答に掲載 | ➡ | 聞き取れない箇所を確認できる！ |

3つの方法で音声が聞けます！

音声再生サービスご利用可能期間

2023年2月24日〜2024年8月31日

※ご利用期間内にアプリやPCにダウンロードしていただいた音声は，期間終了後も引き続きお聞きいただけます。

※これらのサービスは予告なく変更，終了することがあります。

① 公式アプリ「英語の友」(iOS/Android)でお手軽再生

リスニング力を強化する機能満載

- 再生速度変換（0.5〜2.0倍速）
- お気に入り機能（絞込み学習）
- オフライン再生
- バックグラウンド再生
- 試験日カウントダウン

※画像はイメージです。

[ご利用方法]

1. 「英語の友」公式サイトより，アプリをインストール
   https://eigonotomo.com/ 　[英語の友 🔍]
   （右の2次元コードから読み込めます）

2. アプリ内のライブラリよりご購入いただいた書籍を選び，「追加」ボタンを押してください

3. パスワードを入力すると，音声がダウンロードできます
   [パスワード：tpbckw] ※すべて半角アルファベット小文字

※本アプリの機能の一部は有料ですが，本書の音声は無料でお聞きいただけます。
※詳しいご利用方法は「英語の友」公式サイト，あるいはアプリ内ヘルプをご参照ください。

② パソコンで音声データダウンロード (MP3)

［ご利用方法］

1 Web特典にアクセス　詳細は，p.7をご覧ください。

2 「一次試験［二次試験］音声データダウンロード」から
聞きたい検定の回を選択してダウンロード

※音声ファイルはzip形式にまとめられた形でダウンロードされます。
※音声の再生にはMP3を再生できる機器などが必要です。ご使用機器，音声再生ソフト等に関する技術的なご質問は，ハードメーカーもしくはソフトメーカーにお願いいたします。

③ スマートフォン・タブレットでストリーミング再生

［ご利用方法］

1 自動採点サービスにアクセス　詳細は，p.8をご覧ください。
（右の2次元コードから読み込めます）

2 聞きたい検定の回を選び，
リスニングテストの音声再生ボタンを押す

※自動採点サービスは一次試験に対応していますので，一次試験・リスニングの音声のみお聞きいただけます。（二次試験・面接の音声をお聞きになりたい方は，①リスニングアプリ「英語の友」，②音声データダウンロードをご利用ください）
※音声再生中に音声を止めたい場合は，停止ボタンを押してください。
※個別に問題を再生したい場合は，問題番号を選んでから再生ボタンを押してください。
※音声の再生には多くの通信量が必要となりますので，Wi-Fi環境でのご利用をおすすめいたします。

CDをご希望の方は，別売「2023年度版英検2級過去6回全問題集CD」
（本体価格1,200円＋税）をご利用ください。

持ち運びに便利な小冊子とCD3枚付き。※本書では，収録箇所を**CD 1** **1**～**16**のように表示。

Web特典について

購入者限定の「Web特典」を，皆さまの英検合格にお役立てください。

ご利用 可能期間	**2023年2月24日〜2024年8月31日** ※本サービスは予告なく変更，終了することがあります。	
アクセス 方法	スマートフォン タブレット	右の2次元コードを読み込むと， パスワードなしでアクセスできます！
	PC スマートフォン タブレット 共通	1. Web特典（以下のURL）にアクセスします。 　　https://eiken.obunsha.co.jp/2q/ 2. 本書を選択し，以下のパスワードを入力します。 　　**tpbckw** ※すべて半角アルファベット小文字

〈特典内容〉

（1）自動採点サービス
リーディング（筆記1〜3），リスニング（第1部・第2部）の自動採点ができます。詳細は
p.8を参照してください。

（2）解答用紙
本番にそっくりの解答用紙が印刷できるので，何度でも過去問にチャレンジすることができ
ます。

（3）音声データのダウンロード
一次試験リスニング・二次試験面接の音声データ（MP3）を無料でダウンロードできます。
※スマートフォン・タブレットの方は，アプリ「英語の友」（p.5）をご利用ください。

（4）2級面接対策
【面接シミュレーション】入室から退室までの面接の流れが体験できます。本番の面接と同
じ手順で練習ができるので，実際に声に出して練習してみましょう。
【面接模範例】入室から退室までの模範応答例を見ることができます。各チェックポイント
で，受験上の注意点やアドバイスを確認しておきましょう。
【問題カード】面接シミュレーションで使用している問題カードです。印刷して，実際の面
接の練習に使ってください。

自動採点サービスの利用方法

正答率や合格ラインとの距離，間違えた問題などの確認ができるサービスです。

ご利用可能期間	2023年2月24日～2024年8月31日 ※本サービスは予告なく変更，終了することがあります。	
アクセス方法	スマートフォン タブレット	右の2次元コードを読み込んでアクセスし，採点する検定の回を選択してください。
	PC スマートフォン タブレット 共通	p.7の手順で「Web特典」にアクセスし，「自動採点サービスを使う」を選択してご利用ください。

［ご利用方法］

1 オンラインマークシートにアクセスします

Web特典の「自動採点サービスを使う」から，採点したい検定回を選択するか，各回のマークシートおよび問題編の各回とびらの2次元コードからアクセスします。

2 「問題をはじめる」ボタンを押して筆記試験を始めます

ボタンを押すとタイマーが動き出します。制限時間内に解答できるよう，解答時間を意識して取り組みましょう。

3 筆記試験を解答し終わったら，タイマーボタン  を押して
タイマーをストップさせます

4 リスニングテストは画面下にある音声再生ボタンを押して
音声を再生し，問題に取り組みましょう
一度再生ボタンを押したら，最後の問題まで自動的に
進んでいきます。

5 リスニングテストが終了したら，
「答え合わせ」ボタンを押して答え合わせをします

採点結果の見方

タブの選択で【あなたの成績】と【問題ごとの正誤】が切り替えられます。

＜採点結果画面＞

切り替えタブ

【あなたの成績】
🅐 技能ごとの正答率が表示されます。2級の合格の目安，正答率60％を目指しましょう。
🅑 大問ごとの正答率が表示されます。合格ラインを下回る大問は，対策に力を入れましょう。
🅒 採点サービス利用者の中でのあなたの現在位置が示されます。

【問題ごとの正誤】
各問題のあなたの解答と正解が表示されます。間違っている問題については色で示されますので，別冊解答の解説を見直しましょう。

※画像はイメージです。

英検® Information

出典：英検ウェブサイト

英検2級について

2級では，「社会生活に必要な英語を理解し，また使用できる」ことが求められます。
入試，単位認定，さらに海外留学や社会人の一般的な英語力の証明として幅広く活用されています。
目安としては「高校卒業程度」です。

試験内容

一次試験　筆記・リスニング

主な場面・状況	家庭・学校・職場・地域（各種店舗・公共施設を含む）・電話・アナウンスなど
主な話題	学校・仕事・趣味・旅行・買い物・スポーツ・映画・音楽・食事・天気・道案内・海外の文化・歴史・教育・科学・自然・環境・医療・テクノロジー・ビジネスなど

筆記試験　85分

問題	形式・課題詳細	問題数	満点スコア
1	文脈に合う適切な語句を補う。	20問	650
2	パッセージ（長文）の空所に文脈に合う適切な語句を補う。	6問	
3	パッセージ（長文）の内容に関する質問に答える。	12問	
4	指定されたトピックについての英作文を書く。（80〜100語）	1問	650

リスニング　約25分　放送回数／1回

問題	形式・課題詳細	問題数	満点スコア
第1部	会話の内容に関する質問に答える。	15問	650
第2部	短いパッセージの内容に関する質問に答える。	15問	

2022年12月現在の情報を掲載しています。試験に関する情報は変更になる可能性がありますので、受験の際は必ず英検ウェブサイトをご確認ください。

二次試験 面接形式のスピーキングテスト

主な場面・題材	社会性のある話題
過去の出題例	環境に優しい素材・オンライン会議・屋上緑化・ペット産業・新しいエネルギー・サプリメントなど

スピーキング　約7分

問題	形式・課題詳細	満点スコア
音読	60語程度のパッセージを読む。	650
No.1	音読したパッセージの内容についての質問に答える。	
No.2	3コマのイラストの展開を説明する。	
No.3	ある事象・意見について自分の意見などを述べる。 （カードのトピックに関連した内容）	
No.4	日常生活の一般的な事柄に関する自分の意見などを述べる。 （カードのトピックに直接関連しない内容も含む）	

英検®の種類

英検には、実施方式が異なる複数の試験があります。実施時期や受験上の配慮など、自分に合った方式を選択しましょう。なお、従来型の英検とその他の英検の問題形式、難易度、級認定、合格証明書発行、英検CSEスコア取得等はすべて同じです。

▶ 英検®(従来型)
紙の問題冊子を見て解答用紙に解答。二次試験を受験するためには、一次試験に合格する必要があります。

▶ 英検 S-CBT
コンピュータを使って受験。1日で4技能を受験することができ、申込時に会場・日程・ライティングの解答方式が選べます。原則、毎週土日に実施されています（級や地域により毎週実施でない場合があります）。ほかの実施方式で取得した一次試験免除の資格も申請可能です。

▶ 英検 S-Interview
点字や吃音等、CBT方式では対応が難しい受験上の配慮が必要な方のみが受験可能。

受験する級によって選択できる方式が異なります。各方式の詳細および最新情報は英検ウェブサイト（https://www.eiken.or.jp/eiken/）をご確認ください。

合否判定方法

統計的に算出される英検CSEスコアに基づいて合否判定されます。Reading，Writing，Listening，Speakingの4技能が均等に評価され，合格基準スコアは固定されています。

技能別にスコアが算出される！

技能	試験形式	満点スコア	合格基準スコア
Reading（読む）	一次試験（筆記1〜3）	650	
Writing（書く）	一次試験（筆記4）	650	1520
Listening（聞く）	一次試験（リスニング）	650	
Speaking（話す）	二次試験（面接）	650	460

● 一次試験の合否は，Reading，Writing，Listeningの技能別にスコアが算出され，それを合算して判定されます。
● 二次試験の合否は，Speakingのみで判定されます。

合格するためには，技能のバランスが重要！

英検CSEスコアでは，技能ごとに問題数は異なりますが，スコアを均等に配分しているため，各技能のバランスが重要となります。なお，正答数の目安を提示することはできませんが，2016年度第1回一次試験では，1級，準1級は各技能での正答率が7割程度，2級以下は各技能6割程度の正答率の受験者の多くが合格されています。

英検CSEスコアは国際標準規格CEFRにも対応している！

CEFRとは，Common European Framework of Reference for Languages の略。語学のコミュニケーション能力別のレベルを示す国際標準規格。欧米で幅広く導入され，6つのレベルが設定されています。
4技能の英検CSEスコアの合計「4技能総合スコア」と級ごとのCEFR算出範囲に基づいた「4技能総合CEFR」が成績表に表示されます。また，技能別の「CEFRレベル」も表示されます。

CEFR	英検CSEスコア	実用英語技能検定　各級の合格基準スコア					
C2	4000 - 3300	■CEFR算出範囲			B2扱い	C1扱い	1級 満点3400
C1	3299 - 2600			2級 満点2600	準1級 満点3000		合格スコア 2630　3299
B2	2599 - 2300		準2級 満点2400	B1扱い	合格スコア 2304　2599		2304
B1	2299 - 1950	3級 満点2200	A2扱い	合格スコア 1980　2299	1980		
A2	1949 - 1700	A1扱い	合格スコア 1728　1949	1728	CEFR算出範囲外		CEFR算出範囲外
A1	1699 - 1400	合格スコア 1456　1699	1400	CEFR算出範囲外			
	1399 - 0	CEFR算出範囲外　1400	CEFR算出範囲外				

※ 4級・5級は4技能を測定していないため「4技能総合CEFR」の対象外。
※ 詳しくは英検ウェブサイトをご覧ください。

英検®（従来型）受験情報

※「従来型・本会場」以外の実施方式については，試験日程・申込方法が異なりますので，英検ウェブサイトをご覧ください。
※ 受験情報は変更になる場合があります。

◉ 2023年度 試験日程

第1回

申込受付	3月31日 ▶ 5月2日
一次試験	6月 4日（日）
二次試験	A 7月 2日（日）
	B 7月 9日（日）

第2回

申込受付	8月1日 ▶ 9月8日
一次試験	10月 8日（日）
二次試験	A 11月 5日（日）
	B 11月 12日（日）

第3回

申込受付	11月1日 ▶ 12月14日
一次試験	1月21日（日）2024年
二次試験	A 2月18日（日）2024年
	B 2月25日（日）2024年

※ 一次試験は上記以外の日程でも準会場で受験できる可能性があります。
※ 二次試験にはA日程，B日程（2～3級），C日程（1級，準1級）があり，受験級などの条件により指定されます。
※ 詳しくは英検ウェブサイトをご覧ください。

◉ 申込方法

| 団体受験 | ▶ | 学校や塾などで申し込みをする団体受験もあります。詳しくは先生にお尋ねください。 |
| 個人受験 | ▶ | インターネット申込・コンビニ申込・英検特約書店申込のいずれかの方法で申し込みができます。詳しくは英検ウェブサイトをご覧ください。 |

お問い合わせ先

英検サービスセンター

TEL. 03-3266-8311

㈪～㈮ 9：30 ～ 17：00
（祝日・年末年始を除く）

英検ウェブサイト

www.eiken.or.jp/eiken/

試験についての詳しい情報を見たり，入試等で英検を活用している学校の検索をすることができます。

2022年度の傾向と攻略ポイント

2022年度第1回検定と第2回検定を分析し，出題傾向と攻略ポイントをまとめました。2級の合格に必要な正答率は6割程度だと予測されます。正答率が6割を切った大問は苦手な分野だと考えましょう。

一次試験　筆記（85分）

1　短文の語句空所補充

1〜2文程度の長さからなる文の空所に入る適切な語を選ぶ。

問題数 **20問**
めやす **12分**

傾向
- 単語　空所に入る語の品詞は第1回・第2回とも，動詞が4問，名詞が4問，形容詞・副詞が各1問で，通常通りの配分，難易度的にも平均レベルだった。
- 熟語　第1回と第2回ともに主に動詞的表現が出題される傾向にあった。第2回では副詞的表現も比較的多く出題された。
- 文法　(18)〜(20) では通例文法の問題が出題される傾向にあるのだが，今回は，第1回では It is time に続く仮定法過去，第2回では完了形の分詞構文が出題され，それ以外は第1回では but for, had better not, 第2回では as if, There is no telling, といった定型表現的な出題であった。

攻略ポイント
熟語は，動詞的表現が頻出であるが，形容詞的表現，副詞的表現も出題されるので，偏りなく学習しておく必要がある。文法に関しては仮定法，分詞構文が頻出。高校卒業時までの基本的な文法事項は押さえておく必要がある。

2　長文の語句空所補充

[A][B] 2つの長文の空所に最適な語句を補充する。

問題数 **6問**
めやす **18分**

傾向
3段落の長文で，各段落に空所が1つずつある通常通りの問題形式であった。文脈から適切な接続語句を選択する問題と，主語の後に論理的に続く述語部分を答えさせる問題が頻出傾向にある。プラスチック廃棄物に関する問題が第1回，第2回ともに出題された。

攻略ポイント
接続語句の問題，述語部分が空所になっている問題が頻出。接続語句に注意し，文章の論理展開を追っていく練習や，主語の後に論理的にどのような述語がくるのかを考えながら読むことが重要である。日ごろからバラエティに富んだ英文に慣れ親しんでおく必要があるが，特に環境問題は頻出なので注意が必要。

3　長文の内容一致選択

[A][B][C] 3つの長文の内容に関する質問に答える。

問題数 **12問**
めやす **35分**

傾向
[A] は 250 語程度のEメール，[B] と [C] はそれぞれ 360 語程度の論説文である。[A] の設問は3問，[B] の設問は4問，[C] の設問は5問で，ともに1段落につき1つの設問が対応していることが多い。[C] の設問の5問目は「以下の記述のうち正しいのはどれか。」という選択肢から長文の内容と一致するものを選ぶ形式が多い。

攻略ポイント
日ごろから歴史，文化，社会，自然，科学など幅広いトピックの英文に慣れ親しんでおきたい。また，1段落につき1つの設問が対応している傾向があるので，設問を1問ずつ読み，内容を把握したうえで，その答えを段落ごとに探すと効率的である。

4 英作文
指定されたトピックについての英作文を書く。

問題数 **1**問
めやす **20**分

傾向 第1回のトピックは「歴史をより良く理解するためには重要な史跡に行くことが必要だと思うか」、第2回は「日本はもっと外国人労働者を受け入れるべきかどうか」であった。歴史的な話題から社会的な話題まで、さまざまなことに関して意見を問われる傾向にある。

攻略ポイント まず冒頭ではっきりと自分の意見を表明し、その後、自分の意見をサポートする理由や具体例などを述べる。そして最後にもう一度まとめ文として冒頭の意見を再度繰り返す。このような型に沿って英文を書くと論旨が明確になり効果的である。

一次試験 リスニング（約25分）

第1部 会話の内容一致選択 放送される会話の内容に関する質問に対して最も適切な答えを4つの選択肢から選ぶ。　問題数 **15**問

第2部 文の内容一致選択 放送される英文の内容に関する質問に対して最も適切な答えを4つの選択肢から選ぶ。　問題数 **15**問

傾向 第1部は、学校、職場、家庭、店などで交わされる男女の日常会話を聞き取る形式。第2部は、60語程度の英文を聞き取る形式で、トピックは、自然、科学、社会、歴史、文化などのレポート、ある人物の出来事の説明、公共施設や乗り物などでのアナウンス、などが頻出。

攻略ポイント あらかじめ選択肢に目を通し、質問をイメージしておくこと、どうしてもわからない問題は迅速にいずれかの選択肢を選んで次の問題に備えることが重要。トピックとしては上記の傾向から大きく外れたものはあまり出題されないので、このような頻出パターンを日ごろからよく聞いて、素早く理解できるよう練習を積んでおきたい。

二次試験 面接（約7分）

英文（パッセージ）と3コマのイラストのついたカードが渡される。20秒の黙読の後、英文の音読をするよう指示される。それから、4つの質問がされる。

No. 1 カードの英文に関する質問。パッセージの該当箇所を利用して、必要な情報を過不足なく伝えることを心掛けよう。

No. 2 イラストの説明。3コマのイラストを、各コマ2文程度で説明する。矢印の中に書いてある、場所や時間の経過を表す語句で始め（最初のコマでは指定の文をそのまま読めばよい）、それから吹き出しのせりふやイラストの人物の状況や心理を説明する。
ここで、カードを裏返して置くよう指示される。

No. 3 カードのトピックに関係のある事柄についての意見を面接委員が紹介し、それに対してどう思うかを尋ねられる。同意か否かを述べてから、自分の意見を2文程度で述べよう。

No. 4 カードのトピックに関連性のない事柄に関して Yes/No Question で尋ねられる。さらに、Why?/Why not? と理由を尋ねられるので、2文程度で理由を述べよう。

二次試験・面接の流れ

（1）入室とあいさつ

係員の指示に従い，面接室に入ります。あいさつをしてから，面接委員に面接カードを手渡し，指示に従って，着席しましょう。

（2）氏名と受験級の確認

面接委員があなたの氏名と受験する級の確認をします。その後，簡単なあいさつをしてから試験開始です。

（3）問題カードの黙読

英文とイラストが印刷された問題カードを手渡されます。まず，英文を20秒で黙読するよう指示されます。英文の分量は60語程度です。

※問題カードには複数の種類があり，面接委員によっていずれか1枚が手渡されます。本書では英検協会から提供を受けたもののみ掲載しています。

（4）問題カードの音読

英文の音読をするように指示されるので，英語のタイトルから読みましょう。時間制限はないので，意味のまとまりごとにポーズをとり，焦らずにゆっくりと読みましょう。

（5）4つの質問

音読の後，面接委員の4つの質問に答えます。No.1・2は問題カードの英文とイラストについての質問です。No.3・4は受験者自身の意見を問う質問です。No.2の質問の後，カードを裏返すように指示されるので，No.3・4は面接委員を見ながら話しましょう。

（6）カード返却と退室

試験が終了したら，問題カードを面接委員に返却し，あいさつをして退室しましょう。

2022-2

一次試験 2022.10.9 実施
二次試験 A日程 2022.11. 6 実施
　　　　 B日程 2022.11.13 実施

Grade 2

試験時間

筆記：85分
リスニング：約25分

一次試験・筆記　　　　p.18〜32
一次試験・リスニング　p.33〜37
二次試験・面接　　　　p.38〜41

＊解答・解説は別冊p.3〜40にあります。
＊面接の流れは本書p.16にあります。

2022年度第2回

Web 特典「自動採点サービス」対応
オンラインマークシート

※検定の回によって2次元コードが違います。
※筆記1〜3，リスニングの採点ができます。
※PCからも利用できます（本書 p.8 参照）。

一次試験
筆 記

1 次の (1) から (20) までの (　　　) に入れるのに最も適切なものを 1, 2, 3, 4 の中から一つ選び, その番号を解答用紙の所定欄にマークしなさい。

(1) Considering that Keiko has only been studying English for six months, she gave a (　　　) good English presentation at yesterday's contest. She got second prize.
1 remarkably　**2** nervously　**3** suddenly　**4** carefully

(2) *A:* How was your vacation, Dale?
　　B: It was (　　　)! We had seven days of pure fun and relaxation.
1 marvelous　**2** industrial　**3** humble　**4** compact

(3) People around the world are afraid that the (　　　) between the two countries will cause a war.
1 patient　　**2** phrase　　**3** conflict　　**4** courage

(4) The baseball player Shuta Omura had to have (　　　) on his right knee in 2019, but he made a full recovery and was ready to play again in 2020.
1 recognition　**2** innocence　**3** surgery　**4** inquiry

(5) The restaurant lost its good (　　　) after several cases of food poisoning, and eventually it had to close.
1 reputation　**2** anticipation　**3** observation　**4** examination

(6) Sunlight is important for people to stay healthy. However, it is not good to (　　　) skin to too much sunlight.
1 protest　　**2** expose　　**3** conduct　　**4** represent

(7) After Kai broke his arm, it took about three months to (　　　) completely. Now he can play tennis again without any problems.
1 fulfill　　**2** cheat　　**3** heal　　　**4** retire

18

(8) These days, many companies are offering their employees a lot of (   ). For example, staff members can sometimes work from home or choose what time to start and finish.

1 majority　　**2** similarity　　**3** quantity　　**4** flexibility

(9) Kevin got stuck in a snowstorm while driving home. The weather was so bad that he had to (   ) his car and walk the rest of the way.

1 maintain　　**2** abandon　　**3** prevent　　**4** supply

(10) Laura was unhappy about being (   ) from the badminton tournament so early, but now she supports her friends during their matches.

1 committed　　**2** defended　　**3** eliminated　　**4** imported

(11) Sarah has been told to (   ) running until her foot is better. Otherwise, she might make her injury worse.

1 read through　　　　　　**2** refrain from
3 reflect on　　　　　　　**4** refer to

(12) *A:* How did you like the movie?
　　　B: (   ), I enjoyed it. Even though some of the actors weren't the best, the story was great and the music was beautiful.

1 On the move　　　　　　**2** In respect
3 As a whole　　　　　　　**4** By then

(13) *A:* What's wrong, Emily?
　　　B: Jim made a (   ) of me in front of my friends. He said my shoes were ugly.

1 difference　　**2** point　　**3** fool　　**4** start

(14) Jason has asked his mother several times to stop (   ) his personal life. He is upset that she wants to try to control him even though he is an adult.

1 counting on　　　　　　**2** insisting on
3 comparing with　　　　　**4** interfering with

19

(15) *A:* It's a shame that we had to (   ) the barbecue.

　　B: Yes, but we can't hold a barbecue outside in the rain. We can hold it next week instead if the weather is better.

　　1 call off　　　**2** pick on　　　**3** fall for　　　**4** bring out

(16) The thief must have gotten into the building (   ) of a ladder. The only way to get in was through a second-floor window.

　　1 by means　　**2** in charge　　**3** at times　　**4** for all

(17) Barney tried to teach his cat to follow some simple commands, but his efforts were (   ). Every time he told it to lie down, it just walked away.

　　1 of late　　　**2** in vain　　　**3** for sure　　　**4** by chance

(18) (   ) lived in Tokyo for three years, Cassandra knew exactly how to get to Tokyo Skytree from her apartment.

　　1 Having　　　**2** Had　　　**3** Have　　　**4** To have

(19) Somebody had broken one of the windows in Michelle's classroom. Michelle had not done it, but some of the other students looked at her (   ) she had.

　　1 as to　　　**2** as if　　　**3** if only　　　**4** if not

(20) *A:* How long does it take to drive to your parents' house?

　　B: There's no (   ) with traffic during the holidays. It could take thirty minutes, or it could take two hours.

　　1 tell　　　**2** telling　　　**3** tells　　　**4** told

22年度第2回　筆記

（筆記試験の問題は次のページに続きます。）

21

次の英文 [A], [B] を読み，その文意にそって (21) から (26) までの（　）に入れるのに最も適切なものを 1, 2, 3, 4 の中から一つ選び，その番号を解答用紙の所定欄にマークしなさい。

[A]

Trouble at Sea

Plastic is used in a wide variety of goods. In fact, it is estimated that about 400 million tons of plastic is produced around the world each year. Much of it is designed to be used only once and then thrown away. Most of this waste is buried in the ground in landfill sites. However, a large amount (　**21**　). According to the International Union for Conservation of Nature, more than 14 million tons of plastic waste goes into the ocean each year. Plastic is strong and takes a long time to break down. For this reason, the world's oceans are quickly filling up with it.

Plastic waste causes two major problems for wildlife living in and by the ocean. First, animals sometimes get trapped by larger pieces of plastic and die because they are unable to swim freely. The other problem, however, is caused by smaller pieces of plastic. Animals often (　**22**　). A recent study found that about two-thirds of fish species and 90 percent of all seabirds have accidentally eaten tiny pieces of plastic floating in the ocean.

In response, many environmental protection organizations are making efforts to get governments to do something about the plastic in the ocean. For instance, the Center for Biological Diversity has asked the U.S. government to make laws to control plastic pollution. Such groups are also trying to educate the public about the problem. (　**23**　), people continue to throw away plastic, and the amount of plastic in the ocean continues to increase.

22

(21)
1 completely disappears
2 ends up elsewhere
3 is given to charities
4 could be used again

(22)
1 live in large family groups
2 have to make long journeys
3 see these as food
4 leave the ocean

(23)
1 In spite of this
2 Therefore
3 Likewise
4 In particular

[B]

Performing Cats

Andrew Lloyd Webber is famous for writing musicals, and many of the songs he has written have become famous. Over the last 50 years, Webber has created a number of popular musicals, including *The Phantom of the Opera* and *Joseph and the Amazing Technicolor Dreamcoat*. The characters in these were taken from well-known stories that had been around for many years. One of Webber's most successful musicals is *Cats*. This features the song "Memory," the most popular one he has ever written. Like many of Webber's other musicals, though, the characters in *Cats* were (**24**   ).

As a child, one of Webber's favorite books was *Old Possum's Book of Practical Cats* by T. S. Eliot. This is a collection of poems that describe (**25**   ). For example, one of the characters likes to be the focus of everyone's attention. Another seems to be lazy during the daytime, but at night, she secretly works hard to stop mice and insects from causing trouble. Webber used the words of these poems for the songs in his musical, and he created a world in which these cats live together.

Webber began work on *Cats* in 1977, and it had its first performance in London in 1981. It was so popular that it was still being performed there 21 years later. (**26**   ), after its first performance on Broadway in New York City in 1982, it ran for 18 years there. *Cats* has become popular around the world. In fact, the show has been translated into 15 languages, performed in over 30 countries, and seen by more than 73 million people.

24

(24)　**1** not very important
　　　　2 not created by him
　　　　3 difficult to like
　　　　4 based on his friends

(25)　**1** the history of cats as pets
　　　　2 how to take care of cats
　　　　3 the personalities of some cats
　　　　4 how cats' bodies work

(26)　**1** In any case
　　　　2 Unfortunately
　　　　3 By mistake
　　　　4 Similarly

3 次の英文 [A], [B], [C] の内容に関して，**(27)** から **(38)** までの質問に対して最も適切なもの，または文を完成させるのに最も適切なものを **1, 2, 3, 4** の中から一つ選び，その番号を解答用紙の所定欄にマークしなさい。

[A]

From: Michael Green <mikeyg4000@friendlymail.com>
To: Television Depot Customer Service
  <service@televisiondepot.com>
Date: October 9
Subject: ZX950 LCD TV

Dear Customer Service Representative,
After reading several excellent reviews of the ZX950 LCD TV on the Internet, I purchased one from your Television Depot online store. When the item arrived, it appeared to be in perfect condition, and I was able to set it up successfully by following the TV's instruction manual. However, once I started using it, I noticed that there was a problem.
I was unable to adjust the volume of the TV with the remote control. I tried replacing the batteries in the remote control, but this did not fix the problem. I looked through the instruction manual, but I could not find a solution. Although I can adjust the volume with the buttons on the TV, I'm sure that you can understand how inconvenient it is to do it this way.
Would it be possible to obtain a replacement remote control, or do I need to return the TV, too? It would be good if I don't need to send it back because it will be difficult to put such a large TV back into its box. I hope you are able to solve this problem in the next few days. I would very much like to use my new TV to watch the European soccer tournament that begins next weekend. I look forward to receiving your reply.
Regards,
Michael Green

26

(27) What is one thing that Michael Green says about the TV that he bought?

1 It was sent to him without an instruction manual.
2 It has received some positive online reviews.
3 He got it from his local Television Depot store.
4 He chose it because it was in a recent sale.

(28) What problem does Michael Green say the TV has?

1 The sound level cannot be changed with the remote control.
2 The remote control uses up its batteries in just a few hours.
3 The buttons on the TV do not seem to be working.
4 The TV sometimes turns itself off unexpectedly.

(29) Michael Green hopes the customer service representative will

1 send someone to help him put the TV back into its box.
2 solve the problem in time for him to watch a sports event.
3 tell him about tournaments sponsored by Television Depot.
4 give him instructions to allow him to fix the problem himself.

[B] *The Empress's Favorite Clothes*

The Asian country of Bangladesh is one of the largest exporters of clothes in the world. Low wages and modern techniques have allowed clothing factories in Bangladesh to produce cheap clothes. However, until the 19th century, the country produced a luxury cloth called Dhaka muslin. Many regard this cloth as the finest ever made, and it cost over 20 times more than the best silk. It was produced from cotton from a plant called *phuti karpas*. This kind of cotton can be made into very thin threads, which can be used to make incredibly soft and light cloth.

Dhaka muslin was difficult to make, but wealthy people were happy to pay the high prices demanded by the makers. The fame of this cloth spread to Europe, and the wife of Emperor Napoleon of France loved to wear dresses made from Dhaka muslin. When the area that includes Bangladesh became part of the British Empire, though, British traders put pressure on the makers of Dhaka muslin to produce more cloth at lower prices. Eventually, all the makers decided to either produce lower-quality types of cloth or quit.

In 2013, Saiful Islam, a Bangladeshi man living in London, was asked to organize an exhibition about Dhaka muslin. Islam was amazed by the high quality of this material. He wondered if it would be possible to produce Dhaka muslin again. Sadly, he could not find any *phuti karpas* plants in Bangladesh. However, using the DNA from some dried leaves of *phuti karpas* from a museum, he was able to find a species that was almost the same.

Islam harvested cotton from plants of this species, but the threads he made were too thin and broke easily. He had to mix the cotton with some from other plants. The threads made from this mixture, though, were still much thinner than normal. After a lot of hard work, Islam and his team produced some cloth that was almost as good as Dhaka muslin. He wants to keep improving the production technique. The government of Bangladesh is supporting him because it wants the country to be known as the producer of the finest cloth in the world.

(30) What is true of the cloth known as Dhaka muslin?

    1 Its thin threads are over 20 times stronger than those of silk.

    2 It stopped Bangladesh from becoming a major exporter of clothes.

    3 Modern techniques have allowed factories to produce it cheaply.

    4 Many people say it is the best kind that there has ever been.

(31) What happened as a result of the demands made by British traders?

    1 Various colors were introduced to appeal to European customers.

    2 The price of Dhaka muslin in Europe increased dramatically.

    3 Makers began to use British techniques to make better cloth.

    4 Production of high-quality Dhaka muslin stopped completely.

(32) Saiful Islam used the DNA from some *phuti karpas* leaves

    1 to find plants like the ones that were used to make Dhaka muslin.

    2 to check whether samples of Dhaka muslin were genuine or fake.

    3 to explain the evolution of Dhaka muslin at an exhibition.

    4 to create artificial Dhaka muslin in a laboratory in London.

(33) Why is the government of Bangladesh supporting Islam's efforts?

    1 It wants to make the country famous for producing high-quality cloth.

    2 It believes that his project will create new jobs for Bangladeshis.

    3 Because he will quit unless he gets additional financial support.

    4 Because he may discover a way to produce cheap clothes more easily.

[C]
Desert Delight

The Tohono O'odham people are Native Americans who come from the Sonoran Desert. In fact, the name of this tribe means "desert people" in their own language. The Sonoran Desert lies around the border between the United States and Mexico. Traditionally, the Tohono O'odham people lived in villages and grew crops such as beans, corn, and melons. They also ate some of the wild plants and animals that are found in the desert.

Although the Sonoran Desert is hot and dry, it has over 2,000 different species of plants. Hundreds of these plants are safe for people to eat. There are two reasons why the Sonoran Desert has so many species of plants. One is that it contains a variety of types of soil, and these support the growth of many kinds of plants. The other is that, although the desert is mostly dry, it rains a couple of times each year—once in the winter and once in the summer. This rain is enough for some kinds of plants to survive.

One desert plant, the saguaro cactus, is especially important to the people of the Tohono O'odham tribe. Saguaro cactuses can live for over 200 years and grow more than 15 meters tall. Once a year, around June, they produce red fruit. This fruit—the saguaro fruit—has long been a favorite food of the Tohono O'odham people. When the fruit is ready to eat, families work together to knock it down from the cactuses and collect it. The fruit is sweet and delicious when it is fresh, and it can also be turned into sauce or wine so that it can be stored for long periods.

The people of the Tohono O'odham tribe were very independent, and for a long time, they fought to keep their traditional way of life. However, in the early 20th century, the U.S. government forced them to change their lifestyle. It sent Tohono O'odham children to schools to make them learn English and forget their own culture. Many stopped following their traditional way of life. Recently, though, some Tohono O'odham people have begun bringing back their tribe's endangered traditions, including collecting and eating saguaro fruit.

(34) What is true about the Tohono O'odham people of North America?

    1 They used to protect the border between Mexico and the United States.

    2 They lived in small communities and kept farms in a dry area.

    3 They ate wild plants and animals instead of growing their own food.

    4 They were forced to leave their homes and live in the Sonoran Desert.

(35) What is one reason that over 2,000 different types of plants can survive in the Sonoran Desert?

    1 The sunshine in the area means that some plants can actually grow better there.

    2 The Sonoran Desert gets enough rain twice a year to allow the plants to grow.

    3 There are few human beings or wild animals living in the region that eat them.

    4 There is one kind of soil in the desert that almost any plant can grow in.

(36) The saguaro cactus

    1 produces fruit that the local people have enjoyed for a long time.

    2 was discovered by the Tohono O'odham people about 200 years ago.

    3 has roots that grow 15 meters below the ground to reach water.

    4 is best to eat with a special sauce made from traditional wine.

(37) Why did many Tohono O'odham people stop following their traditions?

    1 The U.S. government wanted them to behave more like other U.S. citizens.

    2 The U.S. government offered them opportunities to travel overseas to study.

    3 They wanted their children to study English so that they could enter good schools.

    4 They lost their independence after a war that took place in the early 20th century.

(38) Which of the following statements is true?
1. The method of collecting saguaro fruit is endangering the plants that it grows on.
2. The name of the Tohono O'odham tribe comes from its people's favorite food.
3. The soil in the Sonoran Desert is different in the winter and in the summer.
4. The Tohono O'odham people have a tradition of collecting fruit in family groups.

ライティング
- 以下の TOPIC について，あなたの意見とその<u>理由を 2 つ</u>書きなさい。
- **POINTS** は理由を書く際の参考となる観点を示したものです。ただし，これら以外の観点から理由を書いてもかまいません。
- 語数の目安は 80 語～100 語です。
- 解答は，解答用紙の B 面にあるライティング解答欄に書きなさい。<u>なお，解答欄の外に書かれたものは採点されません。</u>
- 解答が TOPIC に示された問いの答えになっていない場合や，TOPIC からずれていると判断された場合は，<u>0 点と採点されることがあります。</u>TOPIC の内容をよく読んでから答えてください。

TOPIC
Some people say that Japan should accept more people from other countries to work in Japan. Do you agree with this opinion?

POINTS
- Aging society
- Culture
- Language

一次試験
リスニング

2級リスニングテストについて

1　このリスニングテストには，第1部と第2部があります。
★英文はすべて一度しか読まれません。
第1部：対話を聞き，その質問に対して最も適切なものを1，2，3，4の中から一つ選びなさい。
第2部：英文を聞き，その質問に対して最も適切なものを1，2，3，4の中から一つ選びなさい。

2　No. 30のあと，10秒すると試験終了の合図がありますので，筆記用具を置いてください。

第1部　◀))　▶MP3　▶アプリ　▶CD 1 **1**〜**16**

No. 1
1　She lost her map.
2　She is too tired to walk any farther.
3　She cannot find her friend's house.
4　She does not like her neighbors.

No. 2
1　Red wine is her favorite.
2　Her friend does not like French wine.
3　She drank a lot of wine in France.
4　She does not want to spend too much money.

No. 3
1　Call another restaurant.
2　Drive to the supermarket.
3　Make a sandwich for lunch.
4　Go to pick up some food.

No. 4
1　She is sick in bed at home.
2　She gave Eddie her cold.
3　She will leave the hospital in a few days.
4　She got medicine from her doctor.

No. 5
1　He will visit another friend.
2　He has to work on Saturday night.
3　He does not feel well.
4　He is not invited.

No. 6
1 She takes music lessons.
2 She goes bowling with her friends.
3 She helps her cousin with homework.
4 She learns to ride horses.

No. 7
1 A shirt with a bear on it.
2 A soft pillow.
3 A big teddy bear.
4 A bed for her son.

No. 8
1 Changing its soil.
2 Putting it in a bigger pot.
3 Giving it more light.
4 Giving it less water.

No. 9
1 Buy meat.
2 Call his friend.
3 Go to the party.
4 Come home early.

No. 10
1 He will write to the publisher.
2 He will go to another store.
3 He will use the Internet.
4 He will look in his basement.

No. 11
1 She was frightened by a dog.
2 She hurt her leg while running.
3 She walked her dog for a long time.
4 She does not go running often.

No. 12
1 He waits to be told what to do.
2 He is a great history student.
3 He wants to do the report alone.
4 He can be a lazy person.

34

No. 13	1 Their championship parade was canceled.
	2 Their manager is changing teams.
	3 They have not been playing well.
	4 They do not have a nice stadium.

No. 14	1 Somewhere with few people.
	2 Somewhere near his home.
	3 To several cities in Europe.
	4 To a beach resort in Mexico.

No. 15	1 A baseball game is on TV tonight.
	2 The town will build a new town hall.
	3 He should go to the meeting with her.
	4 He should take the children to the park.

第2部 ◀)) ▶MP3 ▶アプリ ▶CD 1 **17**～**32**

No. 16	1 It is too big for her.
	2 It uses too much gasoline.
	3 She needs one that is easier to drive.
	4 She wants one with more doors.

No. 17	1 Some men wore them to look thin.
	2 They could not be worn in England.
	3 Women could not wear them in public.
	4 Wearing them caused pain in people's backs.

No. 18	1 Read comic books at a café.
	2 Clean her kitchen.
	3 Work part-time.
	4 Relax at home.

No. 19

1 It was easy to play at first.
2 It had horses that could fly.
3 She could play with her friend.
4 She could play it several times.

No. 20

1 He had to give information about an accident.
2 He woke up too late to catch his train.
3 He had a problem with his bicycle.
4 He could not find his bicycle in the parking space.

No. 21

1 It was buried together with a prince.
2 It had flower decorations from Siberia on it.
3 It was made by a family in Persia.
4 It had been in one family for many years.

No. 22

1 To move some old things.
2 To clean her kitchen windows.
3 To show her how to use her computer.
4 To help her to do some cooking.

No. 23

1 He saw them being used at an office.
2 He saw an ad for them on the train.
3 He read about them in a magazine.
4 He heard about them from his boss.

No. 24

1 They were decorated with different colors.
2 They were made for different purposes.
3 They were sold at different events.
4 They were served with different meals.

No. 25

1 By the exit on the first floor.
2 By the stairs on the second floor.
3 Next to the computers on the third floor.
4 Next to the cameras on the fourth floor.

No. 26

1 By drinking a lot of donkey milk every day.
2 By washing their bodies with donkey milk.
3 By eating the meat of young donkeys.
4 By spending time looking after donkeys.

No. 27

1 Ask people about their favorite restaurants.
2 Search for a restaurant online.
3 Open a restaurant in her area.
4 Go and take a look at a restaurant.

No. 28

1 Staff will be hired to greet new members.
2 Members can get free protein bars.
3 New exercise machines are coming soon.
4 The fitness center will close in an hour.

No. 29

1 She came home later than she promised.
2 She had forgotten to feed her pet.
3 She had not cleaned the kitchen.
4 She had not done her homework.

No. 30

1 People who bring their pets to the store.
2 People who drive to the supermarket.
3 Customers with a lot of shopping bags.
4 Customers who live less than 5 kilometers away.

問題カード（A日程）　　▶MP3 ▶アプリ ▶CD1 33〜37

A Shortage of Doctors

Nowadays, some parts of Japan do not have enough doctors. It is said that many doctors prefer to work in cities, and this can cause problems for people living in rural areas. A shortage of doctors will prevent these people from receiving good medical treatment, so it is a serious issue. Many people say the government needs to do more about this situation.

Your story should begin with this sentence: **One day, Mr. and Mrs. Kato were talking about going to the beach.**

Questions

No. 1   According to the passage, why is a shortage of doctors a serious issue?

No. 2   Now, please look at the picture and describe the situation. You have 20 seconds to prepare. Your story should begin with the sentence on the card.
<20 seconds>
Please begin.

Now, Mr. / Ms. ——, please turn over the card and put it down.

No. 3   Some people say that young people today do not show enough respect to elderly people. What do you think about that?

No. 4   Today, some young people rent a house and live in it together. Do you think sharing a house with others is a good idea for young people?
Yes.   → Why?
No.   → Why not?

問題カード（B日程） MP3 アプリ CD 1 38〜41

Promoting New Products

Today, some high-quality products are very expensive, so many people worry about whether they should buy them or not. Now, systems that allow people to rent a variety of products monthly are attracting attention. Some companies offer such systems, and by doing so they let people try items before buying them. With such systems, companies can promote their products more effectively.

Your story should begin with this sentence: **One evening, Mr. and Mrs. Kimura were talking about renting a car and going camping by a lake.**

Questions

No. 1   According to the passage, how do some companies let people try items before buying them?

No. 2   Now, please look at the picture and describe the situation. You have 20 seconds to prepare. Your story should begin with the sentence on the card.
<20 seconds>
Please begin.

Now, Mr. / Ms. ——, please turn over the card and put it down.

No. 3   Some people say that, because of electronic money, people will not carry cash in the future. What do you think about that?

No. 4   Some people put solar panels on their houses to produce electricity. Do you think the number of these people will increase in the future?
Yes.   → Why?
No.   → Why not?

2022-1

一次試験　2022.6.5実施
二次試験　A日程　2022.7.3 実施
　　　　　　B日程　2022.7.10実施

Grade 2

> 試験時間

筆記：85分
リスニング：約25分

一次試験・筆記　　　　p.44〜58
一次試験・リスニング　p.59〜63
二次試験・面接　　　　p.64〜67

＊解答・解説は別冊p.41〜78にあります。
＊面接の流れは本書p.16にあります。

2022年度第1回　**Web 特典「自動採点サービス」対応**
オンラインマークシート

※検定の回によって 2 次元コードが違います。
※筆記1〜3，リスニングの採点ができます。
※ PC からも利用できます（本書 p.8 参照）。

一次試験
筆 記

1 次の (1) から (20) までの (　　) に入れるのに最も適切なものを 1, 2, 3, 4 の中から一つ選び，その番号を解答用紙の所定欄にマークしなさい。

(1) Last week, Shelly went to see a horror movie. It was about a strange (　　) that was half shark and half man.
1 creature　　**2** mineral　　**3** package　　**4** instrument

(2) After high school, Ted joined the (　　) so that he could serve his country. He felt proud when he put on his army uniform for the first time.
1 affair　　**2** emergency　　**3** container　　**4** military

(3) Reika's dream is to work for a famous French restaurant in Tokyo. She is trying to (　　) this by going to a cooking school.
1 decrease　　**2** unite　　**3** overwhelm　　**4** accomplish

(4) Arthur was going to sell his café. However, he (　　) his decision because he started to get more customers after a new college opened nearby.
1 abused　　**2** secured　　**3** reversed　　**4** stimulated

(5) Frank did not have (　　) time to write his report, so he asked his boss if he could have a few more days to finish it.
1 possible　　**2** delicate　　**3** financial　　**4** sufficient

(6) There was a fire at a restaurant in Brigston City yesterday. No one was hurt, but the building was (　　) damaged. The owners will have to build a new one.
1 mentally　　　　　　　**2** intelligently
3 annually　　　　　　　**4** severely

(7) Beth was invited to a wedding party last week. She did not want to go by herself, so she asked her friend Jeremy to (　　) her.
1 restrict　　**2** distribute　　**3** accompany　　**4** promote

(8) The SOL-5 rocket will leave Earth tomorrow. The astronauts' (   ) is to repair a weather satellite.

1 foundation   **2** impression   **3** definition   **4** mission

(9) In chemistry class, the students added a small amount of acid to water. Then, they used this (   ) to carry out an experiment.

1 mixture   **2** climate   **3** entry   **4** moment

(10) It was raining very hard in the morning, so the government had to wait to (   ) the rocket into space.

1 elect   **2** impact   **3** sweep   **4** launch

(11) During history class, Aiden noticed that Risa did not have her notebook. He (   ) some paper from his notebook and gave it to her so that she could take notes.

1 tore off   **2** relied on
3 answered back   **4** broke out

(12) Derek (   ) winning his company's golf tournament. However, he played a bad shot on the last hole, and he ended up finishing second.

1 came close to   **2** made fun of
3 took pride in   **4** found fault with

(13) Mr. Griffith warned his students that they would get extra homework if they kept talking in class. He (   ) with his threat because they would not be quiet.

1 followed through   **2** went over
3 got through   **4** turned over

(14) *A:* Guess who I just (   ). Do you remember Gina from college?

   B: Oh, yes. I met her the other day, too. It seems she works in the same building as us.

1 hoped for   **2** ran into
3 looked over   **4** complied with

45

(15) Since changing jobs, Neil has been much more (   ) his work-life balance. He is enjoying his new position, but he is also glad that he can spend more time with his family and friends.

1 separate from   **2** content with
3 based on   **4** equal to

(16) *A:* Mom, is it OK if I invite a couple of friends to the barbecue on Saturday?
B: (   ). There should be more than enough for everyone to eat and drink.

1 In any case   **2** At any rate
3 By all means   **4** On the whole

(17) Alison hates it when her baby brother goes into her room. He always (   ) with her things, and she has to clean up afterward.

1 makes an effort   **2** makes a mess
3 takes a chance   **4** takes a rest

(18) After getting the first prize in the presentation competition, Kevin said in his speech that (   ) for his wife's help, he never would have won.

1 with   **2** but   **3** along   **4** over

(19) Sean has an important meeting early tomorrow morning, so he (   ) better not stay up late tonight.

1 may   **2** would   **3** had   **4** should

(20) *A:* Nicky, you're graduating from high school next year. It's time you (   ) thinking about which university you want to go to.
B: You're right, Dad, but I still don't know what I want to be in the future.

1 started   **2** will start   **3** starting   **4** to start

46

（筆記試験の問題は次のページに続きます。）

2 次の英文 [A], [B] を読み，その文意にそって (21) から (26) までの（　）に入れるのに最も適切なものを 1, 2, 3, 4 の中から一つ選び，その番号を解答用紙の所定欄にマークしなさい。

[A]
An Answer in a Teacup

As in many other countries, people in India are concerned about the problem of plastic waste. After all, the country produces 5.6 billion kilograms of it every year. The system for managing plastic waste needs improvement because a lot of plastic ends up as trash on land and in waterways such as the Ganges River. In response, the Indian government planned to introduce a ban on plastic items that could only be used once. (　**21**　), though, the government was forced to change its plans because of the condition of the economy and worries about an increase in unemployment.

Nevertheless, there is one kind of situation where the use of plastic has come to an end. All 7,000 railway stations in India have replaced plastic teacups with brown clay teacups called *kulhads*. Long before plastic cups were used in India, people enjoyed drinking tea in these traditional cups. The minister for railways in India ordered railway stations to (　**22**　) *kulhads*. By doing so, he hopes the country will take an important step toward ending plastic waste.

There are several reasons why *kulhads* are better than plastic teacups. First, after they have been thrown away, they soon break down into substances that do not harm the environment. Second, the clay that *kulhads* are made from actually improves the flavor of the tea. Finally, using *kulhads* (　**23**　). Plastic cups are made with machines, but *kulhads* are made by hand. The Indian government estimates that hundreds of thousands of people will get extra work because of this change.

48

(21) **1** In the end
2 Moreover
3 For one thing
4 Overall

(22) **1** provide trash cans for
2 use less plastic in
3 only sell tea in
4 charge more for

(23) **1** will create jobs
2 costs less money
3 is better for people's health
4 is just the beginning

[B]
More than Just a Pretty Bird

Parrots are smart and sometimes very colorful birds. They are popular as pets and can often be seen in zoos. Unfortunately, about one-third of parrot species in the wild are in danger of dying out. Examples include hyacinth macaws and Lear's macaws. Each year, some of these birds are caught and sold illegally as pets. (**24**), many are dying because the forests where they live are being cleared to create farmland and to get wood. This has reduced the size of the areas in which they can build nests and collect food.

A study published in the journal *Diversity* revealed that hyacinth macaws and Lear's macaws play an important role in the forests. Researchers studying these parrots in Brazil and Bolivia found that they spread the seeds of 18 kinds of trees. They observed the birds taking fruits and nuts from trees and carrying them over long distances. The birds do this so that they can eat the fruits and nuts later. However, they (**25**). When this happens in areas cleared by humans, the seeds inside the fruits and nuts grow into trees, helping the forests to recover.

Today, conservation groups are working hard to protect hyacinth macaws and Lear's macaws. One difficulty is that these parrots (**26**). An important reason for this is that their eggs are often eaten by other birds. To prevent this, macaw eggs are sometimes removed from their nests by scientists and replaced with chicken eggs. The scientists keep the eggs safe. After the macaw chicks come out of their eggs, they are returned to their parents.

(24) **1** On the contrary
2 Under this
3 What is worse
4 Like before

(25) **1** often go back for more
2 sometimes drop them
3 also eat leaves and flowers
4 bring them to their nests

(26) **1** do not build nests
2 are not easy to catch
3 have poor hearing
4 lose many babies

3

次の英文 [A], [B], [C] の内容に関して, (27) から (38) までの質問に対して最も適切なもの, または文を完成させるのに最も適切なものを 1, 2, 3, 4 の中から一つ選び, その番号を解答用紙の所定欄にマークしなさい。

[A]

From: Noel Lander <noel@coffeeshopsupplies.com>
To: Gary Stein <thedaydreamcoffeeshop@goodmail.com>
Date: June 5
Subject: Your order

Dear Mr. Stein,

Thank you for placing an order by telephone with Jenna Marks of our sales department this morning. The order was for 500 medium-sized black paper cups with your café's name and logo printed on them. According to Jenna's notes on the order, you need these cups to be delivered to you by Saturday.

I am sorry to say that we do not have any medium-sized black coffee cups at this time. What is more, the machine that makes our coffee cups is currently not working. The part that is broken was sent for repair the other day, but it will not be returned to our factory until Friday. Because of this, I am writing to you to suggest some alternatives.

If you really need black cups, then we have them in small and large sizes. However, I guess that size is more important than color for you. We have medium-sized coffee cups in white, and we could print your logo on these instead. We also have medium-sized cups in brown. We are really sorry about this problem. Please let us know which of these options is best, and we'll send you an additional 50 cups for free. Our delivery company says we will need to send the order by Wednesday so that it arrives by Saturday. Please let me know your decision as soon as you can.

Sincerely,
Noel Lander
Customer Support
Coffee Shop Supplies

(27) This morning, Jenna Marks

    1 wrote down the wrong name on Mr. Stein's order.
    2 gave a customer the wrong delivery date.
    3 contacted the sales department by telephone.
    4 took an order for cups for Mr. Stein's café.

(28) According to Noel Lander, what is the problem with the order?

    1 His company does not have the cups that Mr. Stein wants.
    2 His company's machine cannot print Mr. Stein's logo.
    3 The cups cannot be delivered to Mr. Stein until Friday.
    4 The cups were lost by the delivery company the other day.

(29) What does Noel Lander suggest to Mr. Stein?

    1 Ordering more than 50 cups next time.
    2 Using cups that are white or brown.
    3 Offering his customers free coffee.
    4 Buying his cups from another company.

[B]

Tweed

Tweed is the name given to a type of thick cloth that was first developed by farmers in Scotland and Ireland. Long pieces of wool are dyed different colors and then put together to make a cloth with a pattern. The weather in Scotland and Ireland is often cold and wet, so this warm, waterproof material was very popular with the farmers as they worked in the fields.

Tweed did not become well known outside farming communities until the 19th century. At that time, wealthy English people were buying large areas of land in Scotland. These were known as estates, and they were used by their owners for hunting and fishing. Hunters became interested in tweed because it is mainly brown, green, or gray, so wild animals find it difficult to see people wearing clothes made of the material. The wealthy English owners began having patterns of tweed made for their estates. After Queen Victoria's husband, Prince Albert, had a unique pattern made for the people on a royal estate in Scotland, the cloth became famous throughout the United Kingdom.

Clothes made from tweed became standard items for wealthy people to wear in the countryside. Men would wear blue or black suits when doing business in towns and cities, and tweed suits when they went to relax on their estates. Ordinary people began to imitate them by wearing tweed for outdoor hobbies such as playing golf or cycling. The fashion for wearing tweed also spread to the United States and the rest of Europe, and tweed became even more popular in the 20th century when various famous fashion designers used it for their clothes.

Tweed remained fashionable for many years, though by the start of the 21st century, its popularity had dropped. However, tweed is now starting to become popular once more. One reason for this is that it does little harm to the environment. In addition to being made from natural wool, it is strong enough to last for a very long time, so people do not often need to buy new clothes. Indeed, some wealthy people in the United Kingdom still wear their grandparents' tweed suits.

(30) Tweed was popular with farmers in Scotland and Ireland because

  1 it helped keep them warm and dry while they were outside.
  2 it helped them to make some money in their free time.
  3 it allowed them to use any extra wool they produced.
  4 it allowed them to teach their culture to younger people.

(31) How did Prince Albert help to make tweed well-known?

  1 He often went hunting on land owned by farmers in Scotland.
  2 He bought an estate in Scotland where there was a tweed factory.
  3 He was seen wearing it while traveling in Scotland.
  4 He ordered a special tweed pattern for an estate in Scotland.

(32) Ordinary people wore tweed when they were

  1 doing business in towns and cities.
  2 visiting the United States and Europe.
  3 trying to show that they were farmers.
  4 enjoying leisure activities outside.

(33) What is one reason that tweed does little harm to the environment?

  1 It does not release harmful smoke when it is burned.
  2 It does not become dirty easily and needs little washing.
  3 It is tough enough for people to wear it for many years.
  4 It is made by hand in small factories run by families.

[C]
Clues from the Distant Past

Humans who lived before the development of farming left many stone objects behind. These objects are usually parts of tools or weapons, and they show us how these people obtained their food. However, less is known about other parts of their culture. The other source of information we have from this period is paintings on the walls inside caves. These are mostly hunting scenes, so while they show that early humans lived in groups, they do not show that early humans participated in other social activities, such as religious ceremonies.

The lack of evidence led many historians to believe that religions did not develop until humans started to build farms and live in villages. A recent discovery, though, suggests that religious beliefs may have existed before this time. The Shigir Idol is a tall wooden statue that has faces and symbols carved into it. Experts say that it is very likely that these symbols express religious beliefs about the gods they worshipped.

The Shigir Idol was actually found in Russia in 1890. For a long time, people did not know how old it was, but analysis of the wood in the last few years has revealed that it was made around 12,500 years ago—long before humans in the area began farming. The statue was made in several pieces so that it could be taken down and set up again in a different place as the humans who owned it moved around. Unfortunately, some pieces were lost during the early 20th century and only drawings of them remain.

At some point in history, the Shigir Idol fell into a kind of mud that kept it safe for thousands of years. The conditions in which it was found are very rare. Indeed, no other wooden statues of a similar age have been discovered. Judging from the quality of the Shigir Idol, early humans were skilled at making things from wood. However, few wooden items have survived. Despite this, the Shigir Idol has shown historians that early humans had more advanced cultures than people once thought and that they probably also had religions.

(34) What can be learned from the stone objects left behind by early humans?

1 Whether or not they lived in caves.
2 How they were able to get things to eat.
3 Where their groups originally came from.
4 Which kinds of animals they used to hunt.

(35) The Shigir Idol is a wooden statue that

1 has the faces of famous historical leaders carved into it.
2 may show that early humans believed in the existence of gods.
3 is a symbol of the importance of farming to early humans.
4 was probably at the center of one of the first human villages.

(36) What is one thing that has been recently discovered about the Shigir Idol?

1 The humans who owned it made drawings that show how to set it up.
2 Some of the pieces that make up the statue have never been found.
3 The statue can be put together in a number of different ways.
4 It was made by people who had not yet begun growing their own food.

(37) Why is the discovery of the Shigir Idol likely to be a unique event?

1 Because the kind of mud in the area where it was found makes digging difficult.
2 Because early humans often destroyed the religious statues made by other groups.
3 Because few early people had the skills to make something like the Shigir Idol.
4 Because wood survives for thousands of years only in very special conditions.

(38) Which of the following statements is true?

1. The Shigir Idol shows there was cultural exchange between groups of early humans.
2. Paintings in caves show early humans participating in religious ceremonies.
3. Historians have believed for a long time that humans have always had religions.
4. The age of the Shigir Idol was a mystery for many years after it was discovered.

ライティング
- 以下の TOPIC について，あなたの意見とその<u>理由を 2 つ</u>書きなさい。
- **POINTS** は理由を書く際の参考となる観点を示したものです。ただし，これら以外の観点から理由を書いてもかまいません。
- 語数の目安は **80 語〜100 語**です。
- 解答は，解答用紙の **B 面**にあるライティング解答欄に書きなさい。なお，<u>解答欄の外に書かれたものは採点されません。</u>
- 解答が **TOPIC** に示された問いの答えになっていない場合や，**TOPIC** からずれていると判断された場合は，<u>0 点と採点されることがあります。</u>**TOPIC** の内容をよく読んでから答えてください。

TOPIC
Some people say that it is necessary for people to go to important historical sites in order to understand history better. Do you agree with this opinion?

POINTS
- Experience
- Motivation
- Technology

一次試験
リスニング

2級リスニングテストについて

1　このリスニングテストには，第1部と第2部があります。
　★英文はすべて一度しか読まれません。
　第1部：対話を聞き，その質問に対して最も適切なものを 1, 2, 3, 4 の中から一つ選びなさい。
　第2部：英文を聞き，その質問に対して最も適切なものを 1, 2, 3, 4 の中から一つ選びなさい。

2　No. 30 のあと，10 秒すると試験終了の合図がありますので，筆記用具を置いてください。

第1部　　　▶MP3　▶アプリ　▶CD 1 42～57

No. 1
1　When the last train is.
2　How to get to City Station.
3　Whether he can change rooms.
4　What room his clients are in.

No. 2
1　Playing sports with friends.
2　Driving with his mother.
3　Riding his bicycle.
4　Talking to Cathy.

No. 3
1　She took her cat to a hospital.
2　She ran all the way to work this morning.
3　She got up early to clean her kitchen.
4　She had to look for her cat last night.

No. 4
1　He gave his old one to a friend in class.
2　He lost his old one at the aquarium.
3　He needed a bigger one for art class.
4　He wanted one with a different picture on it.

No. 5
1　By cleaning her room.
2　By buying more tissues.
3　By talking to the building manager.
4　By asking her friend for help.

No. 6
1 A chair that will match her desk.
2 A new desk for her room.
3 A wooden shelf for her books.
4 Metal furniture for her room.

No. 7
1 Delivering the mail.
2 Checking his mailbox.
3 Picking up his new license.
4 Getting a package.

No. 8
1 The time of the wedding has been changed.
2 The wedding plans are not finished yet.
3 The honeymoon was not enjoyable.
4 The honeymoon plans were made six weeks ago.

No. 9
1 She is taking a class.
2 She has started her own business.
3 She will call the woman.
4 She moved to a different street.

No. 10
1 She will be working late until next month.
2 She will not speak with Mr. Donaldson.
3 She has never made a presentation before.
4 She has almost finished writing a presentation.

No. 11
1 Wait for Lorie to call.
2 Call Lorie again.
3 Eat dinner at home.
4 Go out with his parents.

No. 12
1 It is the last day of the exhibition.
2 It is nearly closing time.
3 Exhibition tickets will sell out soon.
4 The museum shop is having a special sale.

No. 13
1 She must cook dinner that night.
2 She has to take care of a baby.
3 She is going out with her sister.
4 She will be working late.

No. 14
1 Pay more attention in science class.
2 See Ms. Wilson after school.
3 Work harder in his math class.
4 Try to find a new math tutor.

No. 15
1 Move to Germany.
2 Eat lunch with the man.
3 Find out where the man is going.
4 Have lunch at a good restaurant.

第 2 部　　　　　◀» ▶MP3 ▶アプリ ▶CD 1 58～73

No. 16
1 She did not feel active anymore.
2 Her foot did not get better.
3 There were too many people there.
4 The instructor there was too strict.

No. 17
1 He will hand in reports on Fridays.
2 He will stop working from home.
3 There will be less time to make reports.
4 The staff meeting will move to Wednesdays.

No. 18
1 They wanted to feed it to animals.
2 They needed something sweet to eat.
3 They could not find enough sausages.
4 They did not want to waste animal parts.

No. 19
1 He broke his smartphone.
2 He got lost at night.
3 He had no place to put up his tent.
4 He could not help his friend.

No. 20
1 People from Panama named their country after them.
2 They can keep people's heads warm during winter.
3 Each one takes a long time and special skills to make.
4 There are many colors to choose from.

No. 21
1 By looking for another job.
2 By working less on weekends.
3 By buying less bread.
4 By talking to her manager.

No. 22
1 It would be easier to sell than a car.
2 It would need less space than a car.
3 His wife wanted one to keep in her car.
4 His daughter liked it more than a car.

No. 23
1 By coming to the store early.
2 By introducing a new member.
3 By using the new computers.
4 By buying some coffee.

No. 24
1 She got advice from a lawyer.
2 She was given a yoga mat by a friend.
3 She has been suffering from stress.
4 She plans to write an article about it.

No. 25
1 The soldiers thought zoot suits used too much material.
2 The military used zoot suits when flying in airplanes.
3 The young men did not want to work in suit stores.
4 The businessmen could no longer wear suits.

No. 26
1 There was an advertisement at her school.
2 A teacher told her about a course.
3 She wanted to experience high school life overseas.
4 Her classmates said it would be fun.

No. 27
1 They trade alcoholic drinks for it.
2 They cut open a part of a tree.
3 They buy it at stores in cities.
4 They mix coconut leaves with water.

No. 28
1 Join a party in the lobby.
2 Enjoy free food and drinks.
3 Present flowers to dancers.
4 Hear a 20-minute talk about ballet.

No. 29
1 She will paint the walls.
2 She will remove a cabinet.
3 She will move the fridge.
4 She will get a bigger oven.

No. 30
1 The station opened a new platform.
2 Entrance B2 is closed for repairs.
3 A bag has been found by a staff member.
4 The first floor is being cleaned.

二次試験
面　接

問題カード（A日程）　　　▶MP3 ▶アプリ ▶CD 1 74〜78

Learning about Food

These days, many people are paying more attention to food safety. Because of this, food companies around Japan are trying to let customers know more about their products. Many of these companies use their websites to provide information about how food is produced. Customers check such information, and by doing so they learn more about the food products they purchase.

Your story should begin with this sentence: **One day, Miki was talking to her father in the kitchen.**

Questions

No. 1   According to the passage, how do customers learn more about the food products they purchase?

No. 2   Now, please look at the picture and describe the situation. You have 20 seconds to prepare. Your story should begin with the sentence on the card.
<20 seconds>
Please begin.

Now, Mr. / Ms. ———, please turn over the card and put it down.

No. 3   Some people say that people trust information on the Internet too easily. What do you think about that?

No. 4   Today, there are some Japanese restaurants in foreign countries. Do you think the number of these restaurants will increase in the future?
Yes.   → Why?
No.   → Why not?

65

問題カード（B日程）　　　▶MP3　▶アプリ　▶CD1 79〜82

Protecting Important Sites

Nowadays, more places are being listed as World Heritage sites. However, many natural disasters are happening around the world. Some World Heritage sites have been seriously damaged by them, so they require a lot of work to repair. Communities need to work together to keep World Heritage sites in good condition. It is important to look after such sites for future generations.

Your story should begin with this sentence: **One day, Mr. and Mrs. Ito were talking about their trip.**

Questions

No. 1   According to the passage, why do some World Heritage sites require a lot of work to repair?

No. 2   Now, please look at the picture and describe the situation. You have 20 seconds to prepare. Your story should begin with the sentence on the card.
<20 seconds>
Please begin.

Now, Mr. / Ms. ——, please turn over the card and put it down.

No. 3   Some people say that we should control the number of tourists who visit beautiful places in nature. What do you think about that?

No. 4   Today, many schools give students time to do volunteer activities. Do you think schools should give time for students to do volunteer activities?
Yes.   → Why?
No.   → Why not?

2021-3

一次試験 2022.1.23 実施
二次試験 A日程 2022.2.20 実施
　　　　 B日程 2022.2.27 実施

Grade 2

試験時間

筆記：85分
リスニング：約25分

一次試験・筆記　　　　　p.70〜84
一次試験・リスニング　　p.85〜89
二次試験・面接　　　　　p.90〜93

＊解答・解説は別冊p.79〜116にあります。
＊面接の流れは本書p.16にあります。

2021年度第3回　Web特典「自動採点サービス」対応
オンラインマークシート

※検定の回によって2次元コードが違います。
※筆記1〜3，リスニングの採点ができます。
※PCからも利用できます（本書p.8参照）。

一次試験
筆記

1 次の (1) から (20) までの（　　）に入れるのに最も適切なものを 1, 2, 3, 4 の中から一つ選び，その番号を解答用紙の所定欄にマークしなさい。

(1) A rare bird escaped from the zoo last week. It was finally (　　) today and taken back to the zoo.

1 proved　　　**2** accused　　　**3** captured　　　**4** neglected

(2) *A:* Can you (　　) me to call my mother before we leave on our trip? I mustn't forget.
B: Yes, of course.

1 expect　　　**2** distract　　　**3** remind　　　**4** disturb

(3) Bill was not sure if the new girl was interested in him. He (　　) asked her to go on a date with him and was pleased when she said yes.

1 hesitantly　　　　　　　　**2** academically
3 spiritually　　　　　　　　**4** terribly

(4) *A:* Luke told me that we had about 20 percent more sales than last year. Wendy, can you tell me the (　　) amount?
B: Our sales rose by exactly 21.8 percent.

1 intense　　　**2** endless　　　**3** precise　　　**4** frequent

(5) Good teachers always use (　　) rather than threats to get their students to study.

1 immigration　　　　　　　**2** organization
3 persuasion　　　　　　　　**4** admission

(6) Before Sylvia traveled to Canada, she made sure to get some good (　　) for overseas travel in case something happened to her or her baggage.

1 violence　　　**2** affection　　　**3** insurance　　　**4** punishment

(7) *A:* Was Bob able to help you with your science homework?
B: Actually, he just (　　) me. I couldn't understand his complicated explanations.

1 confused　　　**2** promoted　　　**3** arrested　　　**4** located

70

(8) Although the art gallery wanted to (   ) the painting right away, they had to wait until the owner gave his permission before they could display it.

1 combine   **2** exhibit   **3** imitate   **4** overcome

(9) *A:* Sorry I'm late for class, Ms. Holden. I don't have a good (   ). I just woke up late this morning.
B: Well, maybe you should try going to bed earlier, Stephen.

1 device   **2** excuse   **3** applause   **4** resource

(10) Highway 401 in Canada is the busiest road in North America. Every day, about 420,000 (   ) travel on it.

1 vehicles   **2** tubes   **3** rivals   **4** deserts

(11) The fast-food restaurant (   ) with extra-large drinks because only a few customers ordered them. Now, the drinks are smaller and more customers order them with meals.

1 did away   **2** kept on   **3** went in   **4** got on

(12) *A:* After visiting Kyoto, why don't we go see Sendai tomorrow?
B: Look at the map! Those two places are too far from each other. That won't (   ).

1 live on   **2** account for   **3** cope with   **4** work out

(13) Greg's father taught Greg how to fish, and Greg (   ) plans to teach his son.

1 in turn   **2** in touch   **3** by chance   **4** by heart

(14) After studying law at university, Alex decided to (   ) online crime because he was very interested in computers and the Internet.

1 complain of   **2** specialize in
3 differ from   **4** bound for

(15) Richard's teacher told Richard to stop bothering the other students. She said that if he (   ) behaving badly, she would send him to the principal's office.

1 wore out   **2** persisted in   **3** relied on   **4** made for

71

(16) The power company said that rats were to ( ) the blackout. The animals had eaten through wires connecting houses to the electricity supply.

1 blame for   **2** begin at   **3** add to   **4** act on

(17) Arnold thinks that his daughter ( ) him. Their eyes are the same color, and her nose is a similar shape to his, too.

1 takes after   **2** falls down   **3** lies off   **4** sees in

(18) Misaki's family moved to the United States when she was a little girl. Next year, Misaki ( ) there for more than half of her life.

1 is living   **2** is to live
3 will have lived   **4** has lived

(19) The letter said the bank regretted ( ) Mr. Humphries that his application for a credit card had not been successful.

1 inform   **2** informs   **3** to inform   **4** informed

(20) Chris has been training hard for the city soccer championship. He runs no ( ) than 5 kilometers and spends over an hour exercising in the gym every day.

1 least   **2** less   **3** only   **4** worse

（筆記試験の問題は次のページに続きます。）

次の英文 [A], [B] を読み，その文意にそって (21) から (26) までの（　）に入れるのに最も適切なものを 1, 2, 3, 4 の中から一つ選び，その番号を解答用紙の所定欄にマークしなさい。

[A]

A Feeling for Music

The music of the German composer Ludwig van Beethoven has given happiness to generations of listeners. However, as is well known, Beethoven began to lose his own hearing in his late 20s. By the time he was 44, he was deaf and could hear hardly any sounds at all. (　**21**　), he did not stop writing music, and some of his most famous works were composed after he had lost his hearing.

To celebrate the 250th anniversary of Beethoven's birth, Mate Hamori, the conductor of an orchestra from Hungary, held some special concerts. He invited groups of deaf people to come and enjoy Beethoven's music. In order to "hear" the music, some of the audience members sat next to the musicians and placed their hands on the instruments. By doing this, the deaf people could feel the vibrations made by the instruments as they were being played. Other audience members held balloons which allowed them to feel the music's vibrations in the air. They were able to use (　**22**　) to experience the music.

The concerts were a success. Zsuzsanna Foldi, a 67-year-old woman who had been deaf since she was a baby, cried with joy when she was able to "hear" Beethoven's Fifth Symphony in this way. Although Hamori's idea was unusual, it was not his own. As Beethoven was becoming deaf, he used a piano when writing music. He discovered that the instrument allowed him to feel his music through his fingers. Hamori took Beethoven's idea and used it so that people who (　**23**　) could enjoy the composer's music.

74

(21)   **1** Even so
      2 Rather
      3 For once
      4 Therefore

(22)   **1** this new technology
      2 their sense of touch
      3 the colors of a rainbow
      4 these natural smells

(23)   **1** are unable to leave home
      2 have no memory
      3 face the same challenge
      4 prefer other styles

[B]

Salt Solution

In places with cold winters, snow and ice can cause traffic accidents. To prevent them, salt is often spread on roads in winter. This is done because salt allows ice to melt at temperatures lower than 0°C. For example, a 10 percent salt-water mixture lowers the melting temperature of ice from 0°C to minus 6°C. A 20 percent mixture lowers this temperature further to minus 16°C. However, using salt in this way (24   ). Cars, roads, and even the natural environment can be damaged by salt.

Research has shown that when salt is used on roads, it (25   ). Instead, it is carried into the ground by the melted ice. Much of the salt ends up in lakes and rivers where it can harm underwater plants, fish, and other creatures. High levels of salt can, for example, reduce the size of baby fish by up to one-third. Moreover, salt can lead to an increase in bacteria which not only harm underwater species but also affect the water that people drink.

To avoid these problems, natural alternatives to salt are being tested. One idea has been to use juice from vegetables called beets to melt ice. However, although beet juice is natural, it reduces the amount of oxygen in lakes and rivers, which makes it hard for plants and fish to survive. This is not an easy problem to solve, but researchers are continuing to try different ways to melt ice. (26   ), they will be able to find a substance that can help prevent traffic accidents but does not damage the environment.

(24) **1** changes its flavor
2 is quite common
3 has unwanted effects
4 can be wasteful

(25) **1** soon turns into a gas
2 is eaten by animals
3 cannot be replaced
4 does not just disappear

(26) **1** In reality
2 With luck
3 Like before
4 By then

3 次の英文 [A], [B], [C] の内容に関して，(27) から (38) までの質問に対して最も適切なもの，または文を完成させるのに最も適切なものを 1, 2, 3, 4 の中から一つ選び，その番号を解答用紙の所定欄にマークしなさい。

[A]

From: Amy Gordon <a.gordon@g-kelectronics.com>
To: All Customer Service Staff
    <customerservicestaff@g-kelectronics.com>
Date: January 23
Subject: Staff changes

Dear Customer Service Staff,

I hope everyone enjoyed themselves at the company party last Friday. I had a really good time. I think that the Grand Hotel was the perfect place to have it. Don't forget that some of you won prizes in the bingo games that we played. Steve Miller in the sales department says that he has the prizes, so if you won something, go and see him to pick up your prize.

I have some other announcements as well today. Six new people will be joining our company next month. They've all recently graduated from college, and two of them will be coming to work with us in the customer service department. We'll have three new co-workers altogether because Kent Gardiner will also be moving to our department at the same time. He has worked in the design department at G&K Electronics for 10 years, so I'm sure that many of you already know him.

There are a couple of other staff changes, too. Peter Smith, the manager of the accounting department, will be retiring at the end of next month. Peter has worked at G&K Electronics for over 40 years. There will be a short retirement ceremony for him in Meeting Room A at 5 p.m. on February 28. Also, starting next week, Rachel Martin will take six months off because her baby will be born very soon.

Sincerely,

Amy Gordon
Customer Service Department Manager

78

(27) What did Amy Gordon think of the recent company party?

1 It would have been better if the sales department had been there.

2 It would have been fun to play some bingo games.

3 The prizes this year were nicer than those last year.

4 The choice of location was just right for it.

(28) What is going to happen next month?

1 Some college students will volunteer at the company.

2 Kent Gardiner will move to the design department.

3 Workers at the company will get their first bonus for 10 years.

4 Three people will join the customer service department.

(29) Next week, Rachel Martin will

1 retire from the company after working there for over 40 years.

2 leave work for a while because she will have a child.

3 become the manager of the company's accounting department.

4 be in charge of planning a special event for Peter Smith.

[B]
First Steps

There are two major groups of animals—those which have backbones and those which do not. Animals with backbones are known as vertebrates. The first vertebrates that developed were fish, and for a long time, they were the only vertebrates. Then, around 374 million years ago, some of these fish moved out of the sea and began living on land. These became the first "tetrapods." A tetrapod is a creature which has four limbs—legs and either wings or arms, depending on the kind of animal—and a backbone. Examples of tetrapods include reptiles, birds, and mammals such as human beings.

The movement of vertebrates from the sea to land is considered to be one of the most important events in the history of life on Earth. Even today, though, little is known about exactly how this occurred. One reason for this is that relatively few fossils remain from the time when fish were evolving into tetrapods. The recent discovery of a complete fossil of an ancient fish in Canada, however, has provided new hints about how this change might have happened.

The fossil is of a 1.6-meter-long fish called an elpistostegalian. Scientists have believed for some time that these fish, which looked a bit like crocodiles and lived near the coast, were one of the ancestors of tetrapods. The fish had four fins, two at the front and two at the back, and these may have developed into the four limbs of a tetrapod. The discovery of a complete fossil in Miguasha National Park in Quebec, Canada, has allowed scientists to examine the front fins of an elpistostegalian for the very first time.

The scientists found that the front fins of this ancient fish contained bones like the ones in the hands of land animals. Normally, fins do not contain any bones at all. The scientists believe these bones developed to allow the fish to support its body when it was in shallow water. In other words, the fish began developing hands and feet even before it left the sea. This makes it even more likely that the elpistostegalian is one of the links between fish and tetrapods.

(30) "Tetrapods" are

1 the group of animals that developed into the earliest kinds of fish.

2 the only animals without backbones that have developed arms and legs.

3 animals with a backbone and four limbs which allow them to walk or fly.

4 animals that lived both in the sea and on land about 374 million years ago.

(31) Why are people unsure about how vertebrates first started living on land?

1 Few hints about what the land was like around that time have been found.

2 There is not much fossil evidence from the period when this change happened.

3 Ancient fish fossils show that it occurred in several different ways.

4 Experts are not sure exactly when this important event might have occurred.

(32) The animals called elpistostegalians

1 were a kind of large creature that lived close to land.

2 were early tetrapods that liked to eat crocodiles.

3 developed from tetrapods that had both fins and legs.

4 were unknown to scientists until one was found in Canada.

(33) What did scientists discover when they examined the elpistostegalian fossil?

1 The elpistostegalian's bones were not strong enough for it to survive in deep water.

2 The elpistostegalian's hands and feet must have developed sometime after it left the sea.

3 The elpistostegalian could not have been one of the links between sea and land animals.

4 The elpistostegalian was different from other fish because its fins contained bones.

[C]
An Excellent Fruit

Today, pineapples are one of the world's most popular fruits. For a long time, though, in most parts of the world, they were extremely rare. Pineapples originally come from South America. They first grew in places which are now parts of Brazil and Paraguay. Their natural sweetness made them a favorite of the native people. They were especially popular with the Carib people who lived in coastal areas of South America and on Caribbean islands.

One of the first Europeans to discover pineapples was the explorer Christopher Columbus. On his second voyage to America in 1493, he found some pineapples on the island of Guadeloupe in the Caribbean. He took them back to Spain and presented them to King Ferdinand. At that time in Europe, there was very little sugar, and fruits were only available for short periods during the year. The king tasted a pineapple and declared it to be the most delicious of all fruits. News of this previously unknown fruit quickly spread around Europe.

Unfortunately, the journey from South America to Europe at the time took over a month, so pineapples usually went bad before they reached their destination. Europeans tried to find ways to grow pineapples in Europe instead. The Dutch and the British built greenhouses which were heated to enable pineapples to grow. Huge amounts of fuel were needed to keep the greenhouses warm, and one pineapple took as long as four years to become ready to eat. Growing pineapples became a hobby for very rich people, and pineapples became a status symbol. They were often used as a decoration rather than eaten.

Because of its unusual appearance and status, the pineapple also became a popular image in art and design. Even today, one can find many stone images of pineapples in the gardens of big old houses in Britain. After ships with steam engines were invented, it became much quicker to make the journey from South America to Europe. Pineapple imports grew and prices decreased so that even ordinary people could buy them. As a result, the pineapple lost its luxury image and became a common fruit enjoyed around the world.

(34) Originally, pineapples were

1 hard for many people to get because they only grew in a few places.

2 thought to be too sweet by the native people of South America.

3 introduced to countries like Brazil and Paraguay by the Carib people.

4 used by people on Caribbean islands as food for farm animals.

(35) What happened after King Ferdinand tried a pineapple?

1 He ordered Christopher Columbus to return to America and bring back more.

2 Stories about this unfamiliar but tasty fruit were heard across Europe.

3 European explorers began searching the world for even more delicious fruit.

4 The king realized that people would be healthier if they ate more fruit.

(36) Why did Europeans look for ways to grow pineapples in Europe?

1 In order to become as rich as the people who grew pineapples in South America.

2 In order to stop pirates from attacking their ships and taking their valuable fruit.

3 Because many pineapples were no longer fresh when they arrived in Europe.

4 Because huge amounts of fuel were needed to ship pineapples from South America.

(37) What caused the price of pineapples in Europe to go down?

1 Pineapple farms were created in places closer to Europe than South America.

2 Ships were invented that took less time to travel from South America to Europe.

3 They became so common that ordinary people became tired of eating them.

4 The climate in Britain changed so that people could grow them in their gardens.

(38) Which of the following statements is true?

1 Some people did not want to eat pineapples because their appearance was unusual.
2 Pineapples used to be a way for people to show how wealthy they were.
3 The pineapples that grew naturally in parts of South America were not sweet.
4 Sugar was widely available in Europe at the time of Christopher Columbus.

ライティング
● 以下の TOPIC について，あなたの意見とその理由を 2 つ書きなさい。
● POINTS は理由を書く際の参考となる観点を示したものです。ただし，これら以外の観点から理由を書いてもかまいません。
● 語数の目安は 80 語～100 語です。
● 解答は，解答用紙の B 面にあるライティング解答欄に書きなさい。なお，解答欄の外に書かれたものは採点されません。
● 解答が TOPIC に示された問いの答えになっていない場合や，TOPIC からずれていると判断された場合は，0 点と採点されることがあります。TOPIC の内容をよく読んでから答えてください。

TOPIC
Today in Japan, many buildings and public areas have a lot of lights for decoration, such as the lights used during Christmas. Do you think this is a good idea?

POINTS
● Safety
● The environment
● Tourism

一次試験

リスニング

2級リスニングテストについて

1 　このリスニングテストには，第1部と第2部があります。
　　★英文はすべて一度しか読まれません。
　　第1部：対話を聞き，その質問に対して最も適切なものを 1, 2, 3, 4 の中から一つ選びなさい。
　　第2部：英文を聞き，その質問に対して最も適切なものを 1, 2, 3, 4 の中から一つ選びなさい。

2 　No. 30 のあと，10秒すると試験終了の合図がありますので，筆記用具を置いてください。

第1部　　▶ MP3　▶ アプリ　▶ CD 2 **1**～**16**

No. 1
1　Take him shopping.
2　Pack his boxes.
3　Help him arrange his furniture.
4　Clean his new house.

No. 2
1　To get some medicine.
2　To change his dentist.
3　To get advice over the phone.
4　To make an appointment.

No. 3
1　He will order what she wants to eat.
2　He will change her reservation time.
3　He will go to the restaurant early.
4　He will drive her to the restaurant.

No. 4
1　He should make a new ID.
2　He needs a book for school.
3　He needs to return some books.
4　He cannot use his library card.

No. 5
1　She does not know the time.
2　She does not usually take the bus.
3　She needs to be at work soon.
4　She saw him on the bus.

No. 6

1 It is still at the repair shop.
2 It is connected to the Internet.
3 It has stopped making noises.
4 It has not been working properly.

No. 7

1 She has prepared for her transfer.
2 She knows a lot about Chinese culture.
3 She can speak many languages.
4 She is going to work in China.

No. 8

1 They will buy her something at the mall.
2 They will make her something.
3 They will take her to dinner.
4 They will give her flowers from the garden.

No. 9

1 Go for a horseback ride.
2 Put their bags in their room.
3 Have lunch at the ranch.
4 Check out of their room.

No. 10

1 The parking lot by her shop is closed.
2 The shop next door is too noisy.
3 The man left his things in her office.
4 The man's truck is in front of her office.

No. 11

1 Many hotels in Paris are already full.
2 Traveling to France may become more expensive.
3 A lot of people are going to Paris this summer.
4 Seats on airplanes to France may sell out.

No. 12

1 Some machines need a lot of space.
2 Patients require their own rooms.
3 Every room must have its own machine.
4 Many new doctors will work there.

No. 13	1 The soccer club is only for adults.
	2 There will be practice during summer.
	3 Practice will last for about an hour.
	4 Parents can stay and watch practice.

No. 13
1 The soccer club is only for adults.
2 There will be practice during summer.
3 Practice will last for about an hour.
4 Parents can stay and watch practice.

No. 14
1 He went to the shopping mall.
2 Their car has broken down.
3 They should not go out this afternoon.
4 He cannot fix their stereo.

No. 15
1 He got the wrong kind of medicine.
2 He had to wait a long time at the clinic.
3 He went to see a new doctor.
4 He forgot to go to the clinic.

第 2 部 🔊 ▶MP3 ▶アプリ ▶CD 2 **17**〜**32**

No. 16
1 They have never used a computer.
2 They can type very quickly.
3 They do not want a smartphone.
4 They hope to become teachers.

No. 17
1 They can fly up to 100 kilometers per hour.
2 They can run faster than humans.
3 They make very loud sounds.
4 They make homes near tigers for protection.

No. 18
1 The rent would become less expensive.
2 The building would be closed for construction.
3 He would have to pay an additional charge.
4 He should go to another building during earthquakes.

87

No. 19

1 She knows few people on her soccer team.
2 She will play soccer in a larger league.
3 She is going to meet her favorite soccer player.
4 She has a big soccer match tomorrow.

No. 20

1 It has pictures of castles on it.
2 People use it to make colorful paintings.
3 A king or queen decides who can wear it.
4 Men make it to show their skills to women.

No. 21

1 They were not accepted by a publisher.
2 She hoped they would be made into a movie.
3 The website contacted her and asked for them.
4 Her friends did not have time to read them.

No. 22

1 He knows a lot about some of the events.
2 He knows some of the athletes.
3 He was asked to help by a friend.
4 He was too late to buy any tickets.

No. 23

1 A special novel will be read.
2 It will be a holiday.
3 Old novels will be sold.
4 The floors will be cleaned on Tuesday.

No. 24

1 They were told with more pictures.
2 They were loved more by boys than girls.
3 They were scarier than they are now.
4 They were mostly told by children.

No. 25

1 Her neighborhood is becoming more expensive.
2 Her neighbors have problems with noisy children.
3 Her favorite restaurant is going to close.
4 Her shop will get a new owner soon.

No. 26	1 Looking for a new gym.
	2 Exercising before work.
	3 Going to the gym on his lunch break.
	4 Working at a sports center.

No. 27	1 To announce that a woman will get married.
	2 To tell people about places for short vacations.
	3 To describe a sweet dish eaten at weddings.
	4 To teach couples about married life.

No. 28	1 Get new business cards.
	2 Move desks into a new office.
	3 Make new business plans.
	4 Think of a new company name.

No. 29	1 There were a lot of insects at her school.
	2 She enjoyed being outdoors.
	3 Her friends suggested going camping.
	4 The school trip was canceled.

No. 30	1 By buying 10 hand towels.
	2 By going to the service counter.
	3 By paying for parking every month.
	4 By showing a ticket when they buy things.

面 接

問題カード（A日程）　　　MP3　アプリ　CD 2 33〜37

Healthy Workers

A lot of people in Japan get a medical checkup every year. Some organizations offer a useful service for this. These organizations send special buses that provide medical checkups at the workplace. Many companies use such buses, and by doing so they help busy workers to stay healthy. It is very important that people try to get a medical checkup regularly.

Your story should begin with this sentence: **One morning, Mr. and Mrs. Mori were talking in their living room.**

Questions

No. 1   According to the passage, how do many companies help busy workers to stay healthy?

No. 2   Now, please look at the picture and describe the situation. You have 20 seconds to prepare. Your story should begin with the sentence on the card.
<20 seconds>
Please begin.

Now, Mr. / Ms. ——, please turn over the card and put it down.

No. 3   Some people say that trains and buses in Japan use too much air conditioning in summer. What do you think about that?

No. 4   In Japan, there are many famous brand-name stores. Do you think the number of people who shop at such stores will increase in the future?
Yes.   → Why?
No.   → Why not?

問題カード（B日程）　▶MP3　▶アプリ　▶CD 2 38〜41

Unusual Sea Life

These days, scientists are interested in knowing more about creatures that live deep in the world's oceans. However, reaching areas that are deep in the ocean is very dangerous. Now, some scientists send robots to such areas, and by doing so they can learn about unusual sea life safely. These robots will probably become more and more useful in the future.

Your story should begin with this sentence: **One day, Ken and his mother were talking in their living room.**

Questions

No. 1 According to the passage, how can some scientists learn about unusual sea life safely?

No. 2 Now, please look at the picture and describe the situation. You have 20 seconds to prepare. Your story should begin with the sentence on the card.
<20 seconds>
Please begin.

Now, Mr. / Ms. ——, please turn over the card and put it down.

No. 3 Some people say that we should buy environmentally friendly products even when they are more expensive. What do you think about that?

No. 4 Today, many movies have violent scenes. Do you think people should stop making these movies?
Yes.　→ Why?
No.　→ Why not?

2021-2

Grade 2

一次試験 2021.10.10実施
二次試験 A日程 2021.11. 7 実施
　　　　 B日程 2021.11.14実施

試験時間

筆記：**85分**
リスニング：**約25分**

一次試験・筆記　　　　　p.96〜110
一次試験・リスニング p.111〜115
二次試験・面接　　　　　p.116〜119

＊解答・解説は別冊p.117〜154にあります。
＊面接の流れは本書p.16にあります。

2021年度第2回

**Web特典「自動採点サービス」対応
オンラインマークシート**

※検定の回によって2次元コードが違います。
※筆記1〜3，リスニングの採点ができます。
※PCからも利用できます（本書p.8参照）。

一次試験
筆 記

1 次の (1) から (20) までの (　　) に入れるのに最も適切なものを **1, 2, 3, 4** の中から一つ選び，その番号を解答用紙の所定欄にマークしなさい。

(1) Carrie wants her children to speak more (　　), so she often reminds them to say "please" and "thank you" to other people.
1 luckily　　**2** commonly　**3** politely　　**4** silently

(2) Many people in the United States choose (　　) products instead of foreign ones so as to support American industry.
1 manual　　**2** routine　　**3** domestic　　**4** formal

(3) *A:* I'm going to be away next week, so please (　　) your assignment to Ms. Edwards.
B: OK, Professor Clifton. I'll give it to her as soon as I'm done.
1 submit　　**2** beat　　　**3** convert　　**4** imply

(4) Joe made a web page to sell some of his old items. He put pictures on the web page and wrote a detailed (　　) of each item.
1 route　　　**2** description　**3** hammer　　**4** symphony

(5) The police had (　　) that showed the man had robbed the bank. His face could be seen on a video taken by the bank's security cameras.
1 evidence　　**2** harmony　　**3** rhythm　　**4** praise

(6) Johann's hobby is (　　) music. He wrote a beautiful song for his wife's birthday and played it on the piano at her birthday party.
1 rescuing　　**2** flattering　**3** composing　**4** declaring

(7) Andy focused on (　　) for his science report. It was about how certain birds lost the ability to fly over millions of years.
1 evolution　**2** landscape　**3** humanity　**4** psychology

96

(8) Lisa and her brother had an (   ) about whose turn it was to wash the dishes. They each thought that they were the one who had done it last time.

1 occasion   **2** argument   **3** identity   **4** expense

(9) *A:* I can't get the Internet to work.
B: You need to (   ) that blue cable to the computer. Then it should work.

1 reflect   **2** define   **3** investigate   **4** connect

(10) Kate closed her bedroom window because the sound of the construction on her street was (   ) her.

1 irritating   **2** judging   **3** detecting   **4** exchanging

(11) This morning, Mr. Ikeda was tired at work because he (   ) all night taking care of his baby girl.

1 stayed up   **2** spoke up   **3** left over   **4** looked over

(12) *A:* Do you think $400 will be (   ) three days in New York?
B: No, I think you'll need at least $800. Hotels are expensive there.

1 obliged to   **2** capable of
3 particular about   **4** sufficient for

(13) During his lifetime, the scientist made outstanding contributions to the study of the solar system, to say (   ) of his research in physics.

1 worse   **2** further   **3** better   **4** nothing

(14) *A:* Janet is always complaining about her job.
B: Yeah, I'm getting (   ) of it. I wish she'd stop.

1 low   **2** hard   **3** sick   **4** lazy

(15) Victor cannot be captain of the badminton team anymore because he is too busy with his schoolwork. Michael is going to (   ) as captain.

1 drive off   **2** make sure   **3** pull down   **4** take over

(16) *A:* This car is great, but it costs too much money.

　　　B: Don't worry, honey. Let me see if I can (　　　) the car salesperson into giving us a discount, so we can buy it at a cheaper price.

　　　1 run　　　　　**2** burst　　　　　**3** talk　　　　　**4** divide

(17) George is respected by all the other people in the marketing department. Everyone in his section (　　　) him for his wonderful ideas and hard work.

　　　1 looks up to　　　　　　　　**2** moves on with

　　　3 does away with　　　　　　　**4** takes away from

(18) If Tom's grandparents (　　　) a computer last year, they'd still be using their old typewriter.

　　　1 haven't bought　　　　　　　**2** hadn't bought

　　　3 wouldn't buy　　　　　　　　**4** don't buy

(19) Monica trained very hard for the state tennis championships. (　　　) her efforts, she could not win.

　　　1 Above　　　　**2** Despite　　　　**3** Outside　　　　**4** Within

(20) Shuntaro has always tried to help the other members of the chess club. He has been doing so (　　　) since he became the club's president earlier this year.

　　　1 all the more　　　　　　　　**2** all the best

　　　3 all the better　　　　　　　　**4** all the most

98

（筆記試験の問題は次のページに続きます。）

21年度第2回　筆記

次の英文 [A], [B] を読み，その文意にそって (21) から (26) までの（　）に入れるのに最も適切なものを 1, 2, 3, 4 の中から一つ選び，その番号を解答用紙の所定欄にマークしなさい。

[A]

A Simple Solution

In the town of Burnham-On-Sea in England, police officer Ashley Jones noticed that there were a number of lonely people. He wanted to find a way to make it easier for these people to (**21**). After thinking about the problem, he came up with the idea of turning some of the benches in local parks into "chat benches." He put a sign on each chat bench which says that if someone sits on the bench, that person does not mind having a conversation with a stranger.

Only a few days after he set up the chat benches, Jones was happy to discover that his idea was working. People who had never met before were sitting on the benches and talking to each other. The benches are making a big difference, especially to (**22**). Many of them live on their own and find it difficult to travel to visit family or friends. In fact, some seniors do not have the chance to have a conversation for days or even weeks.

A recent survey found that over 9 million people in the United Kingdom often feel lonely. Many of them find it difficult to make friends because they are scared of speaking to people they do not know. Jones's simple idea provides an easy and attractive way to solve the problem of loneliness. (**23**), chat benches are becoming very popular. More than 40 benches have been set up across the United Kingdom, and the idea is spreading to other countries, such as Australia and the United States.

100

(21) **1** understand technology
2 find new homes
3 start talking to others
4 begin doing exercise

(22) **1** the lives of elderly people
2 the local school students
3 people with pets
4 young parents in the town

(23) **1** Indeed
2 Equally
3 On the contrary
4 For one thing

[B]
Cows Need Friends

Milk production is big business. In North America, for example, one person consumes on average over 150 kilograms of milk every year. To supply the huge amount needed, big farms use machines that automatically feed cows and take their milk. Because (24   ), the cost of producing milk is lower. On such farms, though, it is easy for diseases to spread from one animal to another. This can lead to many cows dying on one farm. As a result, cows are often kept separately from a young age.

Scientists in Canada researched the effects of keeping young cows in this way. They compared such cows with ones that had been kept with another cow. The researchers showed a red plastic container, which the cows had never seen before, several times to each cow. The cows that had been kept in pairs were interested in the container at first but soon ignored it. (25   ), the cows that had been kept alone continued to react as if it was the first time they had seen the container. The researchers concluded that cows kept alone are more sensitive to new things.

This is important news for farmers. If cows cannot get used to the feeding and milking machines, milk production slows down. The researchers believe farmers would have fewer problems with feeding and milking if cows were kept in very small groups, rather than separately. The researchers also say that diseases are not such a big problem for small groups. There should be little risk of (26   ) if only two or three of them are kept together.

(24) **1** each cow is much larger
2 the milk can be kept longer
3 fewer people are needed
4 cheaper food is being used

(25) **1** Later on
2 At last
3 In other words
4 On the other hand

(26) **1** feeding cows too much
2 losing many animals
3 wild animals attacking
4 young cows staying healthy

3 次の英文 [A]，[B]，[C] の内容に関して，**(27)** から **(38)** までの質問に対して最も適切なもの，または文を完成させるのに最も適切なものを 1, 2, 3, 4 の中から一つ選び，その番号を解答用紙の所定欄にマークしなさい。

[A]

From: Robert Mitchell <r.mitchell@wmail.com>
To: Melissa Robinson <m-robinson@matlockpost.com>
Date: October 10
Subject: Application for news reporter job

Dear Ms. Robinson,

I am writing today to apply for the news reporter job at *The Matlock Post*. I recently graduated from college with a degree in English, and I would like to start a career as a news writer. I saw an advertisement for the job in your newspaper last Sunday. I then visited your website, where I saw some instructions for applying by e-mail.

Because I just graduated, I do not have any professional experience yet. However, I wrote for the college newspaper, *The Campus Daily*, for three years. In my third year there, I was also the news editor. *The Campus Daily* is run by the college students, but we published high-quality newspapers every week. During that time, I wrote at least four articles a week for the newspaper. I am attaching one of those to this e-mail. In addition, I am attaching a recommendation letter written by my English professor, Dr. Olson.

I am a very hard worker and I get along well with other people. I also do not mind working extra hours or late at night. If you would like to schedule an interview, please call me at (253) 555-6418. I teach English to private students from 8 a.m. until 3 p.m. on Thursdays, but any other time is fine. Thank you.

Sincerely,
Robert Mitchell

(27) How did Robert Mitchell first learn about the news reporter job?

    1 He read an advertisement for it in the newspaper.

    2 He heard about it from someone at his college.

    3 He saw a posting for it on *The Matlock Post* website.

    4 He received an e-mail about the job from a friend.

(28) Robert Mitchell

    1 worked for a professional newspaper for three years.

    2 is attaching four articles to his job application.

    3 was the news editor at a college newspaper for a while.

    4 often writes letters to one of his professors in college.

(29) What will Robert Mitchell be doing on Thursday this week?

    1 Helping students with English during the day.

    2 Working extra hours late at night for his job.

    3 Meeting with some other people that he knows.

    4 Having an interview with Ms. Robinson for the job.

[B]
Beards in History

The hair that grows on a man's face is called a beard. Hair usually starts growing on boys' faces when they are teenagers and their bodies start producing certain chemicals. The scientist Charles Darwin suggested that men produce beards in order to be appealing to females, and many other scientists have supported this theory. Looking at history, however, it is clear that attitudes to beards have varied greatly from culture to culture.

In many cultures, long beards have been seen as a sign of wisdom. In India, for example, religious leaders have often grown long beards. In ancient Israel, there were strict rules preventing men from shaving or cutting their beards. Many of the men in countries near Israel, though, shaved their faces or kept their beards very short. Some historians believe that the ancient Israelis kept their beards long so they would appear different from people in these other nations.

What is perhaps more surprising is that attitudes to beards have not only varied from culture to culture but also from time to time. The ancient Romans, for example, never shaved their faces until about 100 B.C. Then, beards became unpopular, and for about three centuries, important Romans never had beards. However, beards suddenly became fashionable once more. A similar thing happened later in Europe. Beards became unpopular in the 17th century, and men shaved their faces until around the middle of the 19th century. From that time, men in Europe started to grow long beards again.

In the 20th century, too, beards became unpopular in the 1930s, only to come back again in the 1960s. Recently, beards have become popular again among younger men in Europe and North America. This has led to the creation of "beard clubs." These are groups of men who get together and compare their beards. Some of these clubs decided to start the World Beard and Moustache Championships (WBMC), which are held every two years. In 2017, the WBMC were held in Austin, Texas, and 738 competitors from 33 countries were involved. The event even included competitions for fake beards in which women could participate.

(30) The scientist Charles Darwin

   1 studied how attitudes to beards have changed in different cultures over time.

   2 discovered that certain chemicals make hair grow on the faces of teenage boys.

   3 had the idea that beards are a way for men to be more attractive to women.

   4 supported a theory about beards that was suggested by a group of scientists.

(31) According to some historians, what is one reason men in ancient Israel grew long beards?

   1 Because they did not want to look the same as men in nearby countries.

   2 Because they did not agree with the rules about shaving their beards.

   3 Because they hoped to appear wiser than other people in their community.

   4 Because they were showing their respect for religious leaders in India.

(32) What was surprising about ancient Romans' attitudes to beards?

   1 The Romans thought that important people should not be allowed to grow them.

   2 Roman boys would never shave their faces until they had grown long beards.

   3 Beards were unpopular for around 300 years before becoming popular again.

   4 Their attitudes had an effect on fashions in Europe during the 17th century.

(33) The World Beard and Moustache Championships

   1 led to the creation of a number of beard clubs.

   2 have special categories to allow women to take part.

   3 are held every year in the city of Austin in Texas.

   4 were canceled in the 1930s and returned in the 1960s.

[C]
Ocean Treasure

As economies grow, more goods are manufactured, so there is a constant need for metals. Changes in technology have further increased this demand. For example, computers and smartphones require rare metals such as gold. The amount of metal available on land, however, is limited. It is expensive for mining companies to dig deep into the ground to find metals. For these reasons, mining companies are now looking for metals under the sea.

In the past, finding metals under the sea was considered to be too much of a challenge. In the last few decades, however, places where rare metals can be found have been discovered. These places are called "hydrothermal sea vents." They are created when seawater flows deep inside the earth, where the rocks are very hot. The rocks are made of substances that contain metals. The water absorbs these substances. As the water gets hotter, it rises, pushes through the seafloor, and returns to the ocean. When the hot water mixes with the cold seawater, the substances in it are dropped on the seafloor.

Because they are deep in the ocean, hydrothermal sea vents were not discovered until the 1970s. Scientists are interested in them not only because of the metals they contain, but also because of the amazing creatures found living near them. The water around the vents is very hot, dark, and full of powerful acids. In spite of these difficult conditions, bacteria and animals have adapted to live in these places. Unlike almost all other living things on the planet, these special creatures do not depend on energy from the sun.

The conditions around the vents mean that mining near them is very challenging. The technology to mine close to the vents now exists, but it is still very expensive. There are other problems with deep-sea mining, too. Scientists believe that sometime soon, companies will be able to afford to mine metals from the seafloor. However, mining around the vents would probably harm the creatures that live there. Consequently, although mining the seafloor for metals will become possible, governments and environmental groups might fight against it and perhaps even try to ban it.

(34) Why are more companies looking for ways to get metals from the sea?

1 Changes in technology have made it easy and cheap to do so.

2 The metals needed for manufacturing goods cannot be found on land.

3 There is more demand for certain kinds of metals which are hard to find.

4 They cannot dig any deeper into the ground to find rare metals.

(35) Hydrothermal sea vents

1 began appearing in rocks on the seafloor during the last few decades.

2 are places where seawater heated by rocks under the seafloor comes out.

3 absorb substances containing metals and keep them deep inside the earth.

4 send up rocks from deep inside the earth and drop them on the seafloor.

(36) What is one reason that scientists are interested in hydrothermal sea vents?

1 They contain special metals that were only discovered recently.

2 They are full of powerful acids that are uncommon in the ocean.

3 Unusual animals that do not rely on the sun for energy live there.

4 The heat they create could be used as a source of energy.

(37) What challenges will deep-sea mining probably face in the future?

1 Governments might fight each other for the best deep-sea mining areas.

2 Scientists will have to work hard to invent the technology needed for it.

3 It will cost a lot of money to move the creatures living around the vents.

4 People might try to stop it because of possible damage to the environment.

109

(38) Which of the following statements is true?

1 Finding metals in the ocean was thought to be too difficult to do in the past.
2 New computers and smartphones use smaller amounts of rare metals than old ones.
3 Scientists discovered how to get metals from hydrothermal sea vents in the 1970s.
4 Some countries have made it illegal for companies to carry out deep-sea mining.

ライティング
● 以下の TOPIC について，あなたの意見とその理由を 2 つ書きなさい。
● POINTS は理由を書く際の参考となる観点を示したものです。ただし，これら以外の観点から理由を書いてもかまいません。
● 語数の目安は 80 語〜100 語です。
● 解答は，解答用紙の B 面にあるライティング解答欄に書きなさい。なお，解答欄の外に書かれたものは採点されません。
● 解答が TOPIC に示された問いの答えになっていない場合や，TOPIC からずれていると判断された場合は，0 点と採点されることがあります。TOPIC の内容をよく読んでから答えてください。

TOPIC
It is sometimes said that all people should be able to enter museums for free. Do you agree with this opinion?

POINTS
● Donations
● Learning environment
● Maintenance

一次試験
リスニング

2級リスニングテストについて

1　このリスニングテストには，第1部と第2部があります。
　★英文はすべて一度しか読まれません。
　第1部：対話を聞き，その質問に対して最も適切なものを 1, 2, 3, 4 の中から一つ選びなさい。
　第2部：英文を聞き，その質問に対して最も適切なものを 1, 2, 3, 4 の中から一つ選びなさい。

2　No. 30 のあと，10秒すると試験終了の合図がありますので，筆記用具を置いてください。

第1部　　▶MP3　▶アプリ　▶CD 2 42～57

No. 1
1　Cancel her scuba-diving tour.
2　Take a scuba-diving course.
3　Find a new spot to go diving.
4　Travel to Starfish Island.

No. 2
1　He left something at home.
2　He missed his train.
3　He was late for work.
4　He had to cancel a meeting.

No. 3
1　Learning about Brazil.
2　Buying tropical fish.
3　Going on a fishing trip.
4　Working in a fish market.

No. 4
1　It is going to New York.
2　It is only one hour long.
3　It will arrive in 30 minutes.
4　It will probably arrive early.

No. 5
1　She brings her baby to the office.
2　She wants to continue working.
3　She wants to work full-time.
4　She lives with her parents.

No. 6

1 Open a bank account.
2 Exchange some money.
3 Send some money overseas.
4 Get a new passport.

No. 7

1 His co-worker is having a birthday.
2 His boss will buy him lunch.
3 He has just been promoted.
4 He will be sent to a new city.

No. 8

1 He has collected stamps for a long time.
2 He has some letters to mail.
3 He may start a new hobby.
4 He will go to England soon.

No. 9

1 They should try eating something new.
2 They should cook Thai food for dinner.
3 Meat and potatoes is her favorite meal.
4 Her husband should help out in the kitchen.

No. 10

1 Pay for his tour.
2 Get a visa.
3 Go to a travel agency.
4 Apply for a passport.

No. 11

1 Write about choosing a college.
2 Start getting the newspaper.
3 Check the news on the Internet.
4 Read the article at the library.

No. 12

1 Buy Angie a new plant.
2 Water Angie's plants.
3 Call Angie at work.
4 Pick Angie up at the airport.

No. 13
1 He does not like cheese.
2 He is often away from home.
3 He needs to go somewhere.
4 He wants to order another pizza.

No. 14
1 She does not want to wait.
2 She does not like noodles.
3 She does not feel very hungry.
4 She does not have enough money.

No. 15
1 A new bus station was built near his home.
2 Something is wrong with his car.
3 The buses are always on time.
4 It costs less than driving.

第 2 部　◀)） ▶MP3 ▶アプリ ▶CD 2 58～73

No. 16
1 See a doctor.
2 Go for a long walk.
3 Use the pool at the gym.
4 Climb a mountain.

No. 17
1 To show the main color of the city's flag.
2 To welcome an important guest to the city.
3 Because the builders of the gate liked the color.
4 Because it matches flowers that grow around the city.

No. 18
1 A bus will arrive late.
2 An exit will be closed soon.
3 There has been an accident.
4 To give directions to get to a station.

No. 19	1 She wanted to thank him for his help.
	2 She lost her wallet on her way home.
	3 She needed him to open her door.
	4 She had to tell him about her move.

No. 20	1 It could turn quickly in the air.
	2 It could pull big planes in the air.
	3 It did not need gasoline to fly.
	4 It did not need a pilot to fly.

No. 21	1 He borrowed a smartphone.
	2 He bought a battery charger.
	3 He took a taxi to his office.
	4 He called his customer.

No. 22	1 It was made by a group of artists.
	2 It is a model of a famous artist's home.
	3 It has a grand piano in every room.
	4 It can be lived in by children.

No. 23	1 Borrow money from a bank.
	2 Open a special savings account.
	3 Help his daughters find a university.
	4 Get information about starting a business.

No. 24	1 She is going to make a French dish at home.
	2 She is going to see a movie at a theater.
	3 She is going to eat dinner at a restaurant.
	4 She is going to order pizza and watch movies.

No. 25	1 She got a message about it from a friend.
	2 She saw information about it at a café.
	3 She heard about it from one of her professors.
	4 She read about it at college.

No. 26
1 To water his garden every weekend.
2 To grow some small flowers.
3 To remove some parts of a tree.
4 To plant more grass under a tree.

No. 27
1 To keep shirts closed.
2 To keep pants from falling down.
3 As toys for animals.
4 As decorations for clothes.

No. 28
1 By shopping at the supermarket every month.
2 By buying a set of wine glasses.
3 By signing up for a membership card.
4 By spending more than $60 at the store.

No. 29
1 By doing his laundry every week.
2 By showing him how to order things online.
3 By cleaning his house when he is tired.
4 By cooking for him at her home.

No. 30
1 It will be more windy than usual.
2 It will be cold and rainy.
3 It will be sunny with clear skies.
4 It will be warmer than expected.

二次試験
面 接

問題カード（A日程）　　◀)) ▶MP3 ▶アプリ ▶CD 2 74~78

Quality of Information

Nowadays, a large amount of information is available online. However, some of this information is not based on fact, so demand for information that can be trusted is increasing. People use such information in everyday life, and in this way they can make better decisions about things around them. In the Internet age, the source of information is becoming more important.

Your story should begin with this sentence: **One day, Mr. and Mrs. Ito were talking about selling some things at a flea market.**

Questions

No. 1   According to the passage, how can people make better decisions about things around them?

No. 2   Now, please look at the picture and describe the situation. You have 20 seconds to prepare. Your story should begin with the sentence on the card.
<20 seconds>
Please begin.

Now, Mr. / Ms. ———, please turn over the card and put it down.

No. 3   Some people say that people need to be more careful when shopping on the Internet. What do you think about that?

No. 4   Today in Japan, many trains and buses have signs and announcements in English. Do you think there should also be signs and announcements in other foreign languages?
Yes.   → Why?
No.   → Why not?

117

問題カード（B日程）

Learning about Athletes

Athletes are always trying to improve their performance. Now, there are training centers that can help them do this. These places have special devices to record data about various body movements. Experts study such data, and by doing so they learn about the strong and weak points of athletes. This information can be an important tool for improving athletes' performance.

Your story should begin with this sentence: **One day, Miki and her father were at home.**

Questions

No. 1 According to the passage, how do experts learn about the strong and weak points of athletes?

No. 2 Now, please look at the picture and describe the situation. You have 20 seconds to prepare. Your story should begin with the sentence on the card.
<20 seconds>
Please begin.

Now, Mr. / Ms. ——, please turn over the card and put it down.

No. 3 Some people say that people today put too much personal information on the Internet. What do you think about that?

No. 4 Today, many people ride bicycles in their daily lives. Do you think people have good manners when they use bicycles?
Yes.　→ Why?
No.　　→ Why not?

2021-1

一次試験 2021.5.30 実施
二次試験 A日程 2021.6.27 実施
　　　　 B日程 2021.7. 4 実施

Grade 2

試験時間

筆記：85分
リスニング：約25分

一次試験・筆記　　　p.122〜136
一次試験・リスニング p.137〜141
二次試験・面接　　　p.142〜145

＊解答・解説は別冊p.155〜192にあります。
＊面接の流れは本書p.16にあります。

Web 特典「自動採点サービス」対応
オンラインマークシート

※検定の回によって2次元コードが違います。
※筆記1〜3，リスニングの採点ができます。
※ PC からも利用できます（本書 p.8 参照）。

一次試験

筆 記

1 次の (1) から (20) までの（　　）に入れるのに最も適切なものを 1, 2, 3, 4 の中から一つ選び，その番号を解答用紙の所定欄にマークしなさい。

(1) At first, the marketing department and the sales department were working on the project together. But people in the sales department were too busy, so now the project is being run (　　) by the marketing department.

1 needlessly   **2** entirely
3 scientifically   **4** violently

(2) Experts at the art gallery discovered that one of their paintings, which they had thought was a (　　) Picasso, was actually just a copy.

1 genuine   **2** severe   **3** logical   **4** portable

(3) The musician Jimmy Baker had a lot of (　　) when he was a child. His family was very poor before he became a rich and famous rock star.

1 permission   **2** membership
3 concentration   **4** hardship

(4) Mother Teresa helped many sick people and gave food to many hungry children in India. She was known as a person who cared about (　　).

1 generation   **2** gravity   **3** hesitation   **4** humanity

(5) As Liam walked down the dark street, he began to feel afraid. He had the (　　) that someone was watching him.

1 feature   **2** translation   **3** sensation   **4** property

(6) Risa buys water that comes from a mountain stream. She says that drinking it is good because it has many (　　) that her body needs.

1 campaigns   **2** operations   **3** illustrations   **4** minerals

(7) The lifeguard ran into the ocean to help a young girl who looked like she was (   ) in the big waves.

1 proposing   **2** converting   **3** drowning   **4** exporting

(8) Yesterday was a hot day at the zoo, so Heather bought an ice cream. It melted so quickly that she could not help (   ) some on her dress.

1 arguing   **2** spilling   **3** convincing   **4** maintaining

(9) In the past, sailors had to use the stars to (   ) when they were on an ocean. These days, ships have modern equipment that shows sailors which way to go.

1 satisfy   **2** respect   **3** permit   **4** navigate

(10) Daisuke's grandmother eats a lot of vegetables, drinks green tea, and goes for a long walk every evening to (   ) her health.

1 interpret   **2** replace   **3** preserve   **4** betray

(11) Theresa knew (   ) first sight that Joe was a nice person because he had a gentle smile and kind eyes.

1 in   **2** of   **3** at   **4** to

(12) *A:* I'm thinking of buying Dad some wine for his birthday.
B: Well, he's very (   ) about wine. You'd better ask him what kind he wants.

1 sweet   **2** guilty   **3** enormous   **4** particular

(13) *A:* Sam, what time do you want me to (   ) you off at the movie theater?
B: The film starts at 7:00, so how about 6:45?

1 pick   **2** drop   **3** take   **4** mark

(14) *A:* Excuse me. Is this belt included in today's half-price sale?
B: I'm sorry, sir. The sale does not (   ) belts or wallets.

1 apply to   **2** vote for   **3** put off   **4** tie up

(15) Reika wants a purple kimono. There is a kimono shop in the mall. However, she does not know if she can get one there, so she is going to shop online to find one (   ).

1 for sure   **2** for instance   **3** in short   **4** in vain

(16) A heavy storm (   ) in Montaine Valley last month. The farmers in the area could not sell their vegetables because they were damaged.

1 had some difficulty   **2** did a lot of harm
3 took a break   **4** found fault

(17) When Jocelyn graduates from college, she wants to work for a volunteer organization. She wants to spend her time working (   ) other people.

1 at the sight of   **2** for a change of
3 for the benefit of   **4** at the thought of

(18) *A:* What time does our train leave?
B: In 20 minutes. It's time we (   ) for the station.

1 left   **2** have left   **3** had left   **4** will have left

(19) It was so noisy at the concert that Jane struggled to (   ). She had to shout to communicate with her friend.

1 make heard herself   **2** make herself heard
3 hearing herself made   **4** herself made heard

(20) Mr. Martinez is loved by all the students in the school. However, Ms. Garcia is not (   ) as he is, so she is less popular than Mr. Martinez.

1 as kind a person   **2** a kind as person
3 as a kind person   **4** as person a kind

124

（筆記試験の問題は次のページに続きます。）

次の英文 [A], [B] を読み，その文意にそって (21) から (26) までの (　　) に入れるのに最も適切なものを 1, 2, 3, 4 の中から一つ選び，その番号を解答用紙の所定欄にマークしなさい。

[A]
Self-Sufficient Communities

Recently, many people have been trying to change their lives in order to (　21　). One way they do this is by choosing products that create less pollution, such as vegetables that have been grown without using chemicals. Also, by buying from local producers, they reduce the amount of fossil fuel needed to transport products. Some people even join "self-sufficient communities." In these communities, people work together to produce everything they need to live—food, clothes, furniture, fuel, and medicines.

In the 1970s, an Englishman named John Seymour promoted the idea of self-sufficiency. He had spent much of his life (　22　). For example, he went to South Africa and managed a sheep farm. While he was there, he spent time with local people who taught him how to find food in the wild. He also made a journey from Europe to India, observing how different agricultural communities lived. These experiences gave Seymour the idea of trying to get away from cities, offices, and factories.

Seymour published a book in 1976 which explained how to do things like growing crops and keeping bees. At the time, the book inspired thousands of people to join self-sufficient communities. However, most of these people found the lifestyle challenging, and they had given up by the early 1980s. Now, though, the idea is attracting interest again. Many young people are turning away from city life and becoming farmers. This time, many of them have decided not to be completely self-sufficient. (　23　), they are using modern technology to earn enough money to buy things that are difficult to produce themselves.

126

(21)
1 spend more time away from work
2 bring home more money
3 be kinder to the environment
4 become stronger and healthier

(22)
1 traveling and learning about farming
2 living and working on big ships
3 studying to become a great chef
4 writing about interesting cultures

(23)
1 At last
2 Meanwhile
3 Like before
4 Rather

[B]
Masters of the Desert

"Bedouin" is a name given to some of the people who live in North Africa and the Middle East. Unlike most people, many Bedouins do not (**24**). Instead, they are nomads, which means that they are always moving about. They walk around the hot deserts of countries like Egypt and Israel, leading their camels and sheep to grass and water. Life in the desert is not easy, but over thousands of years, Bedouins have developed unique skills to help them survive.

Some people estimate that there are around 20 million Bedouins in the world today. However, (**25**). Because many of them are traveling, it is impossible to count them all. In recent years, however, many Bedouins have given up their traditional way of life. This is because the amount of land controlled by governments has increased, which has made it harder for the Bedouins to travel freely. Some of them now live in urban areas and have regular jobs, such as driving taxis and working in restaurants.

Some Bedouins have found work with the Israeli army as trackers. A tracker is a person who follows people by using signs left on the ground, such as the marks left by feet or tires. Trackers must know their environment well and be quick to notice anything unusual. (**26**), with their desert survival skills, Bedouins are excellent trackers. About 1,600 of them are now serving in the Israeli army, and their ability to notice dangers along Israel's borders is helping to protect the country.

(24) **1** sleep lying down
2 live in one place
3 eat meat or fish
4 use paper money

(25) **1** their exact numbers are unknown
2 there were many more in the past
3 the groups have no government
4 they all meet once every year

(26) **1** Naturally
2 Occasionally
3 Secondly
4 Equally

次の英文 [A], [B], [C] の内容に関して，(27) から (38) までの質問に対して最も適切なもの，または文を完成させるのに最も適切なものを 1, 2, 3, 4 の中から一つ選び，その番号を解答用紙の所定欄にマークしなさい。

[A]

From: Peter Decker <p-decker@yourworldls.org>
To: Feng Li <feng.li@mymail.com>
Date: May 30
Subject: Teaching Chinese

Dear Ms. Li,

Thank you for your interest in teaching at the Your World Language School in London. During your online interview, we thought you had some great ideas for making learning fun and exciting for children, and we would like to offer you a position teaching Chinese at our school. The official start date for the position is August 1, but we would like you to attend a two-week training program here before then.

As you know, our language school offers classes to students of all ages, and each lesson is designed to help students achieve their unique goals. Your experience of teaching children will certainly be a big advantage. However, our Chinese program is also very popular with businesspeople, so I would like you to become familiar with that area of teaching as well.

The school will cover your moving costs up to £1,500. Expenses like airline tickets and hotel stays are covered, but food and other personal expenses are not. You will need to submit all original receipts along with the form attached to this e-mail. Also, please look over the attached contract of employment, which describes your work duties, and let me know if you have any questions. We are really looking forward to having you join our team!

Sincerely,
Peter Decker

130

(27) Before starting her job at Your World Language School, Ms. Li must

  1 have an online interview with Peter Decker.
  2 receive training for two weeks in London.
  3 come up with fun ideas for teaching children.
  4 teach some trial Chinese lessons at the school.

(28) What does Peter Decker ask Ms. Li to do?

  1 Design lessons for classes of all ages.
  2 Learn about teaching business Chinese.
  3 Get some experience of teaching children.
  4 Become familiar with the area near the school.

(29) What will Your World Language School do for Ms. Li?

  1 Send her details about her work duties.
  2 Reserve her flight tickets and hotel.
  3 Cover her food and personal expenses.
  4 Help pay for her to move to London.

[B]

In the Air

In many of the world's large cities, air pollution is a serious problem. According to experts, about 7 million people around the world die every year from the effects of dirty air. London, the capital city of the United Kingdom, is one example of a city with this problem. London is said to have some of the worst levels of air pollution in the world. However, because much of this pollution cannot be seen, few people are asking the government to take action to improve the situation.

A man called Pierre Duquesnoy, though, came up with a way to make people more aware of the problem. Duquesnoy's idea was to use a team of pigeons—a bird common in many big cities—to measure levels of air pollution and send the results to a website. At first, Duquesnoy thought about using drones, but he was told that it was against the law to fly drones in London. After that, he realized he could use pigeons instead.

Over a million pigeons are estimated to live in London. They are not popular with residents because they make a mess on buildings and public places. The pigeons that Duquesnoy decided to use were not ordinary pigeons, but homing pigeons. These pigeons have an amazing ability to find their way back from the place where they are released to the place where they live, so they have been used since ancient times for sending messages. Duquesnoy used these pigeons because he could be sure that they would return to their homes and not just fly away.

With help from an expert, Duquesnoy put together a team of pigeons. A small device was attached to the back of each pigeon. These devices measure gases in the air and send the results to a website. During the project, people could look at the website and see where each pigeon was and the level of air pollution in that area. The website had many visitors, and they began to discuss Duquesnoy's project and the problem of air pollution. As a result, more people are saying that the government should do more to clean up London's air.

(30) In London in the United Kingdom,

1 the government is looking at new ways to deal with pollution.

2 the quality of the air is worse than in many other large cities.

3 over a million people die every year from the effects of dirty air.

4 a new kind of pollution has been damaging people's eyes.

(31) What is one reason that Pierre Duquesnoy decided to use pigeons for his project?

1 Pigeons are not as affected by high levels of air pollution as other birds.

2 Pigeons are cheap to use because they are common in many big cities.

3 He found out that using drones in the city of London was not allowed.

4 He thought that using birds would make more people interested in his project.

(32) What is special about the pigeons that Duquesnoy used?

1 They are less likely to make a mess on buildings and public places.

2 They can deliver messages to people living all over London.

3 They have been used since ancient times to perform amazing tricks.

4 They have the ability to find their way back to their homes.

(33) What has happened because of Duquesnoy's project?

1 More people have started talking about the dangers of air pollution.

2 Visitors to London have been using his devices to measure pollution.

3 The government has promised to do more to clean up London's air.

4 Experts have begun using pigeons to collect data about other problems.

[C]
Building a Better Future

Estonia is a country in northern Europe. Before World War II, it was an independent country, but by the end of the war, it was part of the Soviet Union. In those days, there was a shortage of houses in many parts of the Soviet Union, so the government built many apartment buildings. These were meant to be temporary homes, and they were not designed or built well. After the Soviet Union broke up in 1991, Estonia and other countries became independent again. Most of these countries have been destroying their old apartment buildings.

Estonia, however, is turning its apartment buildings into environmentally friendly homes that use energy efficiently. The project began in 2016 with 17 apartment buildings in Tartu, a city in the south of the country, and is known as SmartEnCity. Estonia is now a member of the European Union (EU), and it received financial help from the EU for the project. The aim is not only to reduce the amount of energy consumed by the apartments, but also to turn them into modern, good-looking homes.

Work on the 17 apartment buildings in Tartu has now been completed. Changes have been made to prevent heat from escaping through the walls and windows. A new, efficient heating system has been added. Each apartment has a control panel which lets residents monitor and control the amount of energy they consume. As a result, the residents now use 80 percent less gas to heat their apartments. Also, solar panels have been installed on the buildings, and these produce three times more electricity than the residents need.

Some critics said the project would be a waste of money. However, so far, it seems to be working. The EU paid for half of the cost, and the rest was paid for by residents using money borrowed from banks. The residents are spending less than they used to on energy bills, so they have extra money to repay the loans. Moreover, the work on the apartments has improved the way the city looks. The Estonian government hopes to upgrade some of the other 6,000 old apartment buildings in the country in a similar way.

(34) By the end of World War II,

1 there were empty apartment buildings in many parts of the Soviet Union.

2 Estonia had lost its independence and become part of the Soviet Union.

3 most people in Europe were living in temporary apartment buildings.

4 many people in northern Europe had left their countries to find new homes.

(35) What is one of the goals of the SmartEnCity project?

1 To teach people in Tartu how to make their homes environmentally friendly.

2 To improve old apartment buildings so that they are more energy-efficient.

3 To provide financial help for poor people in a city in the south of Estonia.

4 To reduce the amount of energy used to build houses in the European Union.

(36) What is the control panel in the apartments in Tartu for?

1 It allows people to see and change how much energy they are using.

2 It reduces the amount of heat escaping through the walls of the apartments.

3 It controls the amount of electricity produced by the solar panels.

4 It lets residents choose whether to use gas or electricity to heat their apartments.

(37) How are residents of the apartments helping to pay for the project?

1 By helping to upgrade 6,000 similar apartment buildings.

2 By using money that would have been spent on bills.

3 By carrying out many of the improvements themselves.

4 By working for the European Union to pay for half of the cost.

(38) Which of the following statements is true?

1 The SmartEnCity project has helped to turn Tartu into a more attractive city.
2 The European Union gave money to build 17 new apartment houses in Estonia.
3 Countries decided to leave the Soviet Union because of housing shortages.
4 Over 80 percent of gas consumption in Estonia is for heating private homes.

ライティング
●以下の TOPIC について，あなたの意見とその理由を 2 つ書きなさい。
●POINTS は理由を書く際の参考となる観点を示したものです。ただし，これら以外の観点から理由を書いてもかまいません。
●語数の目安は 80 語～100 語です。
●解答は，解答用紙の B 面にあるライティング解答欄に書きなさい。なお，解答欄の外に書かれたものは採点されません。
●解答が TOPIC に示された問いの答えになっていない場合や，TOPIC からずれていると判断された場合は，0 点と採点されることがあります。TOPIC の内容をよく読んでから答えてください。

TOPIC
It is often said that restaurants and supermarkets should try to reduce the amount of food that they throw away. Do you agree with this opinion?

POINTS
● Cost
● Health and safety
● The environment

一次試験
リスニング

2級リスニングテストについて

1 このリスニングテストには，第1部と第2部があります。
★英文はすべて一度しか読まれません。
第1部：対話を聞き，その質問に対して最も適切なものを 1, 2, 3, 4 の中から一つ選びなさい。
第2部：英文を聞き，その質問に対して最も適切なものを 1, 2, 3, 4 の中から一つ選びなさい。

2 No. 30 のあと，10秒すると試験終了の合図がありますので，筆記用具を置いてください。

第1部 ▶MP3 ▶アプリ ▶CD3 1〜16

No. 1
1 Shop at a flea market.
2 Watch a play.
3 Go fishing with the man.
4 Drive to Bakersville.

No. 2
1 He will be showing his cousin around.
2 He will visit his boss in the hospital.
3 He will have lunch with his friend.
4 He will be working late.

No. 3
1 Order a gift catalog.
2 Help his mother buy a gift.
3 Ask the woman for a gift idea.
4 Look for a gift somewhere else.

No. 4
1 Using an old helmet.
2 Studying in the library alone.
3 Riding her bike home at night.
4 Being late for class.

No. 5
1 He cannot find it.
2 He is away until then.
3 He is still reading it.
4 He does not have to pay a fee.

No. 6	1 He got it at a cheap electronics store.
	2 He hopes the woman will buy it.
	3 It has too much data on it.
	4 It does not work anymore.

No. 7	1 Get help from the girl.
	2 Help the girl study for a test.
	3 Have more tough tests.
	4 Get a private teacher.

No. 8	1 Talk to a college employee.
	2 Go to the shopping mall.
	3 Look for a bank on campus.
	4 Use an ATM across the street.

No. 9	1 He can start working again soon.
	2 He should come back tomorrow.
	3 He needs to take more pills.
	4 He has to get another x-ray.

No. 10	1 They will camp in the mountains.
	2 They usually travel by airplane.
	3 They have moved to California.
	4 They are too busy to travel.

No. 11	1 Getting some sleep during the daytime.
	2 Eating lunch more slowly.
	3 Going to bed 20 minutes earlier.
	4 Working until late at night.

No. 12	1 Show her some pictures of his trip.
	2 Give her some magazines.
	3 Make a hotel reservation for her.
	4 Take her around in Thailand.

No. 13
1 There have been many sunny days.
2 There was a mistake in the weather report.
3 The rainy season seems worse than usual.
4 The rainy season started a week ago.

No. 14
1 A bigger place to live.
2 Some time off from work.
3 A less expensive apartment.
4 Some help with their housework.

No. 15
1 He left his ticket at home.
2 He is not old enough.
3 It is sold out already.
4 It is not being shown at the theater.

▌▌▌▌ 第 2 部 ▌▌▌▌▌▌▌▌▌▌▌▌▌▌▌▌▌▌▌▌▌ ◀» ▶MP3 ▶アプリ ▶CD 3 **17**～**32**

No. 16
1 She found an old bicycle.
2 She helped a man near a station.
3 She took a bus back from her office.
4 She went for a walk with her neighbor.

No. 17
1 She called them and told them about it.
2 She showed it to them on a train.
3 They saw it in pictures sent by her.
4 They heard about it at an amusement park.

No. 18
1 Many ships are made there.
2 A warm ocean meets a cold one there.
3 Visitors damage the beautiful beaches there.
4 The daily temperature changes quickly there.

No. 19
1 Visit stores to see products.
2 Go to a customer center.
3 Send an e-mail on Sunday.
4 Look for answers on a website.

No. 20
1 It has been read in many countries.
2 It has been translated into their language.
3 It was brought to Lebanon in 1923.
4 It was used to learn about Western countries.

No. 21
1 She did not like the design of her old ones.
2 She could not read well with her old ones.
3 She lost her old ones at school.
4 She left her old ones in Osaka.

No. 22
1 There are not enough staff members today.
2 There are no computers that can use the Internet.
3 There is a problem with the Internet service.
4 There is a show before the next event.

No. 23
1 Many cities needed strong plants in parks.
2 Factory workers from England took it abroad.
3 Cotton plants grew easily in many factories.
4 Strong material could be made from it.

No. 24
1 Change her workdays.
2 Start work early on Fridays.
3 Work late every Wednesday.
4 Take piano lessons on weekends.

No. 25
1 By sending an application in the mail.
2 By logging in to a smartphone application.
3 By talking to the event staff.
4 By going to the Parkville mall.

No. 26
1 Her friend works at a ballet theater.
2 Her dance teacher recommended it.
3 She saw a program about dancers on TV.
4 She had a picture taken with dancers.

No. 27
1 By selling things he does not need.
2 By canceling his trip to Germany.
3 By borrowing money from his father.
4 By teaching students to play the guitar.

No. 28
1 Her house is too small for her.
2 The area she lives in is getting too noisy.
3 There are no stores near her house.
4 She does not like the animals in her area.

No. 29
1 The afternoon is too hot for a marathon.
2 The roads are not quiet enough in the afternoon.
3 The hotels have special breakfasts in winter.
4 The buildings look good at sunrise.

No. 30
1 The suit he wanted to wear was too small.
2 The suit he wanted to wear was not clean.
3 He could not find the suit he wanted to wear.
4 He left the suit he wanted to clean at home.

21年度第1回　リスニング

問題カード（A日程） ▶MP3 ▶アプリ ▶CD 3 33〜37

A New Type of Service

Nowadays, many people are interested in having a pet. However, when pets become sick or get hurt, the cost of medical treatment can be high. To deal with this, it is a good idea for pet owners to get insurance that covers pets' medical costs. Some companies offer such insurance, and by doing so they try to meet the needs of pet owners.

Your story should begin with this sentence: **One day, Yumi and her father were talking in their car.**

Questions

No. 1 According to the passage, how do some companies try to meet the needs of pet owners?

No. 2 Now, please look at the picture and describe the situation. You have 20 seconds to prepare. Your story should begin with the sentence on the card.
<20 seconds>
Please begin.

Now, Mr. / Ms. ——, please turn over the card and put it down.

No. 3 Some people say that having a pet can help people reduce their stress. What do you think about that?

No. 4 Today, many students take part in club activities at school. Do you think club activities are an important part of school education?
Yes. → Why?
No. → Why not?

問題カード（B日程）

New Ways to Communicate

Today, people have many chances to talk with foreigners. Now, electronic devices that translate languages are becoming more popular. Some hospitals are introducing such devices, and by doing so they are helping foreign patients speak with doctors more easily. However, while new technology is helping people communicate, it is still important that people take the time to try to learn a foreign language.

Your story should begin with this sentence: **One evening, Mr. and Mrs. Fukuda were talking about traveling to France.**

Questions

No. 1   According to the passage, how are some hospitals helping foreign patients speak with doctors more easily?

No. 2   Now, please look at the picture and describe the situation. You have 20 seconds to prepare. Your story should begin with the sentence on the card.
<20 seconds>
Please begin.

Now, Mr. / Ms. ——, please turn over the card and put it down.

No. 3   Some people say that, in the future, Japanese movies will become more popular in foreign countries. What do you think about that?

No. 4   In Japan, a lot of students wear school uniforms. Do you think schools should make students wear uniforms?
Yes.   → Why?
No.   → Why not?

21年度第1回 面接

2020-3

一次試験 2021.1.24実施
二次試験 A日程 2021.2.21実施
　　　　　B日程 2021.2.28実施

Grade 2

試験時間
筆記：85分
リスニング：約25分

一次試験・筆記　　　　p.148〜162
一次試験・リスニング p.163〜167
二次試験・面接　　　　p.168〜171

＊解答・解説は別冊p.193〜228にあります。
＊面接の流れは本書p.16にあります。

2020年度第3回

Web特典「自動採点サービス」対応
オンラインマークシート

※検定の回によって2次元コードが違います。
※筆記1〜3，リスニングの採点ができます。
※PCからも利用できます（本書p.8参照）。

一次試験
筆 記

1 次の **(1)** から **(20)** までの（　　）に入れるのに最も適切なものを **1, 2, 3, 4** の中から一つ選び，その番号を解答用紙の所定欄にマークしなさい。

(1) **A:** It looked like you were enjoying the party, Don. I saw you laughing a lot.
B: Yeah. Rachel was telling some really (　　) stories about her father.
1 marine **2** amusing **3** native **4** silent

(2) **A:** How many people work at your company, Mr. Seward?
B: We (　　) have 30 employees, but we plan to hire 5 more at the end of the year.
1 seriously **2** instantly **3** currently **4** especially

(3) The computers in the library should be (　　) for school projects or homework. Students are not allowed to use them for playing games or watching videos on the Internet.
1 utilized **2** satisfied **3** flavored **4** reflected

(4) In Franklin City, water (　　) has become a big concern. The city is asking people to use as little water as possible.
1 conservation **2** publication
3 revolution **4** ambition

(5) In science class, students learn the names of the (　　) that can be found in nature. They have to know that CO_2 is made of carbon and oxygen.
1 duties **2** narrations **3** witnesses **4** elements

(6) After Susan got married, she chose to keep working at the same company, but on a part-time (　　).
1 rating **2** sense **3** basis **4** charge

(7) **A:** Did people at the art show like your paintings?
B: Yes. I got a lot of (　　). One person said they were the most beautiful paintings he had seen in a long time.
1 mysteries **2** detectives
3 compliments **4** structures

148

(8) *A:* How much does it cost to travel to Dubai?

B: Well, the prices (　　　). They are high over the new year holidays but much lower at other times of the year.

1 vary **2** navigate **3** pause **4** struggle

(9) Karen (　　　) her time between working at a bank and taking care of her children. She would like to spend more time at home, but she also needs to make money.

1 publishes **2** divides **3** scratches **4** attaches

(10) *A:* Kevin, did you call the hotel to (　　　) my reservation for tomorrow?

B: Yes, Ms. Harris. They said you can check in anytime after two o'clock.

1 distinguish **2** confirm **3** promote **4** govern

(11) *A:* I'm thinking of visiting Kyoto in August.

B: Really? You should wait until November. Kyoto is (　　　) then. The weather is cool and the autumn leaves are beautiful colors.

1 behind its back 　　　 **2** against its will
3 at its best 　　　 **4** in its opinion

(12) *A:* When is Uncle Steven going to arrive?

B: He could be here (　　　), so please go and change your clothes.

1 in a series 　　　 **2** for a living
3 at any moment 　　　 **4** to some extent

(13) Sarah spent the summer traveling in Europe with her friends. It was a lot of fun, so she was very sad when it (　　　) an end.

1 dug up **2** came to **3** took over **4** fell on

(14) It is difficult for many students to decide (　　　) a university to enter after high school.

1 under **2** in **3** on **4** beyond

(15) When Wakako was a young girl, she used to do ballet every day. These days, she only does it (　　　) because she is very busy.
1 up and down
2 now and then
3 all the way
4 not at all

(16) Victor likes his new job because he is always (　　　). He uses taxis, trains, and airplanes every day to visit clients all around the country.
1 above all else
2 out of place
3 at a distance
4 on the go

(17) Becky was (　　　) her low test scores, so she did not want to speak to any of her friends at college on Friday.
1 ashamed of
2 rid of
3 accustomed to
4 familiar to

(18) Breakfast (　　　) to be the most important meal of the day. Experts say that it gives people the energy they need to get through the day.
1 has said　　**2** says　　**3** is saying　　**4** is said

(19) It is because the Bluestreet Girls sing and dance so well (　　　) they are so popular with teenagers.
1 that　　**2** if　　**3** how　　**4** why

(20) *A:* This project is going to be very difficult and expensive, Mr. Ford. (　　　) cancel it?
B: No. It will make a lot of money for the company later.
1 What about　**2** What for　　**3** How come　**4** Why not

（筆記試験の問題は次のページに続きます。）

次の英文 [A], [B] を読み，その文意にそって (21) から (26) までの (　) に入れるのに最も適切なものを 1, 2, 3, 4 の中から一つ選び，その番号を解答用紙の所定欄にマークしなさい。

[A]

Cycles of Change

The bicycle is an efficient means of transportation. It was invented in the 19th century, and since then, it has been improved many times. Recently, electric bicycles, or "e-bikes," have become widely used. Unlike a regular bicycle, an e-bike has a motor, which allows the rider to go up hills more easily. Some cycling fans think that it is "cheating" to use a bike with a motor. Nevertheless, e-bikes are quickly (　**21**　). In fact, e-bike sales in the United States were eight times greater in 2018 than in 2014 according to one survey.

Researchers say this is good news. They claim that e-bikes may have a positive effect on people's health and the environment. One major advantage of e-bikes is that older people and those who do not exercise regularly can cycle. This makes it easier for them to commute to work by bike, which is better for the environment than traveling by car. (　**22**　), e-bikes allow more people to cycle as a hobby. People who could not ride along rough roads or up mountains, for example, can now do so.

Some cycling experts, however, point out problems with the increased use of e-bikes. For one, riders of e-bikes are more likely to be involved in accidents. In response, some people want speed limits to be lowered and other measures to increase safety, such as bike paths. Most importantly, experts say riders of both e-bikes and regular bikes should be careful. It does not matter if a bike has a motor or not. The important thing is to enjoy cycling (　**23**　).

(21) 1 reducing electricity use
2 causing new problems
3 growing in popularity
4 improving the environment

(22) 1 What is more
2 Therefore
3 By contrast
4 Despite this

(23) 1 during the warm months
2 together with friends
3 in order to keep fit
4 while staying safe

[B]
A Good Way to Save Space

In recent years, farmers in many countries have been finding it more and more difficult to produce enough food to feed everyone. One reason for this is changes in weather patterns caused by global warming. As global temperatures increase, many places have become too hot and dry to be used for agriculture. (24   ), there is increasing pressure to produce renewable energy, such as solar power. The problem with solar power, though, is that solar panels take up a lot of space. To solve both these problems at once, researchers have recently come up with a way to combine solar power and crop production.

One common challenge in farming is that a lot of direct sunlight (25   ). Not only can it cause the leaves to turn brown and dry, but the heat from the sunlight also quickly dries up the water in the ground. This means that the plants do not get enough water to survive. The researchers decided to set up solar panels at about 2.5 meters above the ground. These created a space with shade for plants and also reduced the amount of water that dried up, which helped to increase crop production.

The solar panels were also able to benefit from the crops. Solar panels do not perform well (26   ). However, crops like lettuce and kale create a cooling effect, which stops the solar panels from overheating and allows them to work more efficiently. The results of this research show that it is possible to produce more food, save space, and enjoy the benefits of solar power.

(24) **1** Without this
2 At the same time
3 After a while
4 Indeed

(25) **1** damages crops
2 is difficult to find
3 attracts more insects
4 makes vegetables taste bad

(26) **1** at high temperatures
2 near cool water
3 under large trees
4 on cloudy days

3 次の英文 [A], [B], [C] の内容に関して, (27) から (38) までの質問に対して最も適切なもの, または文を完成させるのに最も適切なものを 1, 2, 3, 4 の中から一つ選び, その番号を解答用紙の所定欄にマークしなさい。

[A]

From: Mark Tucker <mtucker@berktonmiddle.edu>
To: Margaret Lawson <margaret-lawson8@umail.com>
Date: January 24
Subject: Sylvia's math grades

Dear Ms. Lawson,
This is Mark Tucker, your daughter's math teacher at Berkton Middle School. I wanted to talk to you a little about Sylvia's math grades. I know Sylvia had a bad cold a couple of weeks ago, so she missed a few classes. Unfortunately, the students learned some very important things during that week.
I sent Sylvia's homework to her while she was absent from school, but she missed some important explanations about triangles during the class. She said she understood the topic, but she did very poorly on yesterday's test. I know that this is not her fault. However, it is very important for her to learn this topic. If she doesn't, she will have trouble in the future because we will use the concepts again in the next chapter.
I am available for half an hour before school begins to help students who are having trouble with their schoolwork. Also, math students from West Bridgeville College come to the school library to give free tutoring every Wednesday after school. Sylvia says that you take her to school and pick her up every day. Which would be more convenient for you? Please send me an e-mail and let me know if you'd like to bring Sylvia in earlier or pick her up later on Wednesdays.
Sincerely,
Mark Tucker

156

(27) A couple of weeks ago, Sylvia

    1 started going to Berkton Middle School.
    2 received a bad grade in math class.
    3 got a new math teacher at school.
    4 was not well enough to attend classes.

(28) What is it important for Sylvia to do?

    1 Explain about triangles to the class.
    2 Study harder for tests in the future.
    3 Understand a topic from math class.
    4 Read the next chapter carefully.

(29) What does Mark Tucker want Sylvia to do?

    1 Read some books in the school library.
    2 Get some extra help with her math studies.
    3 Ask her mother to help with her homework.
    4 Go to West Bridgeville College for special lessons.

[B]
Hagfish

The oceans contain many strange and mysterious creatures. One example is the hagfish. Hagfish look like snakes or eels, but their mouths are a special shape, and they have teeth on their tongues. They live deep in the ocean and eat the bodies of fish that have died and sunk to the ocean floor. A hagfish fossil has been found that is 330 million years old. Scientists who study evolution think hagfish are the ancestors of all creatures with backbones, including human beings.

In most countries, few people have heard of hagfish. In South Korea, however, hagfish are used in a popular dish. Their meat is cooked in oil and then served with salt. In particular, older Korean men enjoy eating hagfish while drinking alcohol. This has led to overfishing in Asia. As a result, other countries, such as the United States, have begun catching hagfish in their seas and exporting them to Korea. Hagfish skin is also used to make bags, boots, and other products.

Hagfish have a special way of protecting themselves from animals that attack them, such as sharks. Hagfish produce a thick liquid which is full of thin fibers. When hagfish are attacked, they shoot out this liquid from small holes in the sides of their bodies. When the liquid mixes with seawater, it rapidly expands, turning into a kind of jelly. This jelly protects the hagfish by making it difficult for the fish that is attacking it to breathe.

Douglas Fudge and a group of scientists at the University of Guelph in Canada have seen a possible use for this hagfish liquid. They say that the fibers in the liquid are like very strong silk. They believe that these could be used to replace artificial fabrics, such as nylon, which are made from fossil fuels. The hagfish fibers would be much more environmentally friendly. These scientists are now trying to create similar fibers in the laboratory in order to make a new fabric that is both very strong and light. Clothing manufacturers would be interested in using such a high-quality fabric for their products.

(30) Which of the following is true about hagfish?

1 Other fish swim to deep areas of the ocean in order to catch them.

2 People and many other animals may actually have evolved from them.

3 They are the ancestors of all modern fish that do not have backbones.

4 They are a type of snake that does not have any teeth or a tongue.

(31) People in the United States have started catching hagfish because

1 their meat has become more and more popular among Americans.

2 Koreans use oil taken from hagfish to make health products.

3 other types of more popular fish have already been overfished.

4 their numbers in Asia have declined since too many were caught.

(32) How do hagfish protect themselves from other fish?

1 By expanding their bodies so that they appear much larger.

2 By shooting out thin fibers that make holes in the bodies of other fish.

3 By releasing a liquid from their bodies that changes in seawater.

4 By covering other fish with a jelly that makes it hard to see.

(33) What benefit might hagfish provide in the future?

1 They could be used to develop a material that is better for the environment.

2 They could break down nylon fibers that are polluting the sea.

3 They could help clean up fossil fuels that spill in laboratories.

4 They could be easily changed to produce very strong silk for the fashion industry.

[C]
Recycling Old Ideas

Today, people often recycle items to prevent them from being thrown away in landfills. Recycling metals, in particular, is important because when metals are produced from natural rocks, much harm is caused. Not only is land damaged when taking resources out of the ground, but also many poisons are released into the environment. Furthermore, large amounts of electricity are used. For these reasons, people are looking for ways to recycle metals instead.

Recycling metals actually has a long history. It has always been much easier to reuse metals than to produce them. Metals like iron, copper, and tin are common, but they are difficult to separate from the rocks in which they are found. This is why, in ancient times, Roman armies took metal statues from other countries after wars and melted the statues down to make new weapons. Even as late as the 18th century, Americans were encouraged to donate iron items to be recycled for George Washington's army.

During the 19th century, large companies specializing in recycling were established to meet a higher demand for metals. However, in the 20th century, producing metals became faster and more efficient. Around this time, many product makers began to change the way they increased their profit. Instead of reducing production costs as usual, they started using an approach called "planned obsolescence." This means making products that are designed to break or become unusable after a short period of time, so customers have to buy products more frequently.

These days, such items include devices like smartphones, which must be replaced every few years. They also contain many rare metals. In fact, Americans put around $60 million worth of gold and silver into landfills each year just by throwing away used phones. Although many people already see the importance of recycling large appliances such as refrigerators and washing machines, some do not understand why smaller electronics should be recycled. The amount of metal in the world is limited, so it may be better to learn from old ideas to preserve the world's supply.

(34) What is one way producing metals damages the environment?

1 A lot of living things need metals from the ground in order to survive.

2 A lot of the electricity that is used in the process causes fires.

3 The majority of metals are thrown away and take up space in landfills.

4 The process leads to the release of dangerous substances.

(35) Why did people melt down metal items in the past?

1 Because weapons were needed for wars against the United States.

2 Because it was easier than separating new metals from rock.

3 In order to mix them with rocks to make them stronger.

4 In order to reuse them to make new statues of their war heroes.

(36) During the 20th century,

1 people started to make companies that specialized in recycling.

2 it became faster and more efficient to use metals to make money.

3 product makers made more money by reducing production costs.

4 businesses began to make goods that quickly became useless.

(37) How can people preserve the supply of rare metals?

1 By trying to recycle small electronics instead of throwing them away.

2 By replacing their old phones with ones that run more efficiently.

3 By increasing the number of large appliances used for recycling.

4 By leaving devices that contain gold and silver in landfills.

(38) Which of the following statements is true?

1 George Washington introduced the idea of recycling iron to the United States.
2 There was an increase in the need for metals during the 19th century.
3 Metals can reduce the amount of poisons released by electricity production.
4 Companies spend about $60 million each year on gold for new smartphones.

ライティング
● 以下の TOPIC について，あなたの意見とその理由を 2 つ書きなさい。
● POINTS は理由を書く際の参考となる観点を示したものです。ただし，これら以外の観点から理由を書いてもかまいません。
● 語数の目安は 80 語～100 語です。
● 解答は，解答用紙の B 面にあるライティング解答欄に書きなさい。なお，解答欄の外に書かれたものは採点されません。
● 解答が TOPIC に示された問いの答えになっていない場合や，TOPIC からずれていると判断された場合は，0 点と採点されることがあります。TOPIC の内容をよく読んでから答えてください。

TOPIC
Some people say that more apartment buildings should allow pets such as dogs and cats. Do you agree with this opinion?

POINTS
● Cleanliness
● Lifestyles
● Neighbors

一次試験
リスニング

2級リスニングテストについて

1　このリスニングテストには，第1部と第2部があります。
　★英文はすべて一度しか読まれません。
　第1部：対話を聞き，その質問に対して最も適切なものを1, 2, 3, 4の中から一つ選びなさい。
　第2部：英文を聞き，その質問に対して最も適切なものを1, 2, 3, 4の中から一つ選びなさい。

2　No. 30のあと，10秒すると試験終了の合図がありますので，筆記用具を置いてください。

第1部　▶MP3　▶アプリ　▶CD 3 42～57

No. 1
1　He is going to meet his wife's father.
2　He and his wife will visit his grandmother.
3　He and his wife will take her on a trip.
4　His wife is going to have a baby.

No. 2
1　Getting a job at a restaurant.
2　Lending him some money.
3　Having dinner together.
4　Going on a trip to Peru together.

No. 3
1　It takes an hour to get there.
2　It has some walking trails.
3　It will not be open today.
4　It is located nearby.

No. 4
1　It is inexpensive.
2　It is in a good location.
3　It has a pretty garden.
4　It is bigger than the other houses.

No. 5
1　His teacher announced it in science class.
2　He heard about it from her mother.
3　He asked his mother about it.
4　His school newspaper had a story on it.

No. 6
1. Return after four o'clock.
2. Drive more slowly.
3. Park in a parking lot.
4. Change her parking sticker.

No. 7
1. He was looking after his son.
2. He was away on a business trip.
3. He has been feeling ill.
4. He went on a vacation.

No. 8
1. They have studied German before.
2. They look forward to new adventures.
3. They are not happy about moving to Germany.
4. They do not like food from abroad.

No. 9
1. Look for recipes.
2. Make spaghetti.
3. Go shopping.
4. Clean the bathroom.

No. 10
1. She wants to watch them again soon.
2. She wants to find out his opinion of them.
3. She forgot which ones she lent him.
4. She forgot the ending of *Lost in Brazil*.

No. 11
1. Put them on her desk.
2. Hand them to her.
3. Deliver them to another building.
4. Take them back to his pizza shop.

No. 12
1. It does not sell video games.
2. It is too violent for children.
3. It only sells new items.
4. It is not on sale yet.

No. 13	1 It will start at 6:00.
	2 It will finish a little early.
	3 It will be longer than usual.
	4 It will be held at a different field.

No. 14	1 Sell his hard drive to the woman.
	2 Have his computer repaired.
	3 Work at Computer Plaza.
	4 Get a new computer.

No. 15	1 Her new teacher is strict.
	2 The school offers free classes.
	3 She will start studying Chinese.
	4 Learning Chinese is easier than she thought.

第 2 部   ◀)) ▶ MP3 ▶ アプリ ▶ CD 3 58～73

No. 16	1 He did not like the food his mother had made.
	2 He could not eat all his food.
	3 She had left her lunch at home.
	4 She had given him a snack from the cafeteria.

No. 17	1 They are expected to become the champions.
	2 They are going to start training next month.
	3 They will go to Capton City next week.
	4 They have been preparing overseas.

No. 18	1 To promote a traditional kind of music in Florida.
	2 To teach people about new kinds of instruments.
	3 To protect people while they are underwater.
	4 To help people learn about marine life.

No. 19	1 He will study only on the weekends.
	2 He will study for four hours every day.
	3 He will start studying in the mornings.
	4 He will start studying earlier in the evenings.

No. 20	1 People in Egypt cook it in special pots.
	2 It can be kept and eaten for a long time.
	3 Scientists find new types of it every day.
	4 Over 3,000 pots of it were found in pyramids.

No. 21	1 Make costumes for comic book events.
	2 Start a website about comic books.
	3 Sell her collection of comic books.
	4 Join a comic book fan club.

No. 22	1 A $2,000 discount.
	2 A discount on snow tires.
	3 A weekend trip for a family.
	4 A chance to be on a TV show.

No. 23	1 He took her on a trip this summer.
	2 He took her to swimming lessons.
	3 He bought her some new toys.
	4 He bought her some summer clothes.

No. 24	1 By spending $25 at the gym.
	2 By joining a boxing class.
	3 By introducing two new members.
	4 By coming to the gym every day for a month.

No. 25	1 He does not like staying at hotels.
	2 He does not want to go to Thailand.
	3 He likes going to the beach.
	4 He is interested in temples.

No. 26
1 Watch many documentaries.
2 Interview 15 movie directors.
3 Start writing fantasy stories.
4 Make a movie about real people.

No. 27
1 They live in dangerously high places.
2 They like to go near people.
3 They are considered to be dangerous.
4 They have shorter legs than most birds.

No. 28
1 His boss wants him to transfer.
2 His office in Canada is closing.
3 He got a new job in an office there.
4 He wants to be near his mother.

No. 29
1 It is a place where people have business meetings.
2 It is a gift given to friends and co-workers.
3 It is a time to relax and chat.
4 It is a type of coffee from Sweden.

No. 30
1 Playing for a new soccer team.
2 Training young soccer players.
3 Coaching his old teammates.
4 Managing a new club.

問題カード（A日程）　　　◀» ▶MP3 ▶アプリ ▶CD 3 74〜78

Improving Safety

Natural disasters such as storms and floods can cause serious damage. To stay safe, people need to get information about disasters. Now, the Japanese government offers such information in different languages, and by doing so it tries to improve the safety of foreign visitors to Japan. With the increase of foreign visitors, it is becoming more important to provide services for them.

Your story should begin with this sentence: **One day, Mr. and Mrs. Okuda were talking in their living room.**

Questions

No. 1   According to the passage, how does the Japanese government try to improve the safety of foreign visitors to Japan?

No. 2   Now, please look at the picture and describe the situation. You have 20 seconds to prepare. Your story should begin with the sentence on the card.
<20 seconds>
Please begin.

Now, Mr. / Ms. ——, please turn over the card and put it down.

No. 3   Some people say that high school students in Japan should learn a foreign language in addition to English. What do you think about that?

No. 4   Nowadays, a lot of people go to gyms to exercise in their free time. Do you think the number of these people will increase in the future?
Yes.   → Why?
No.   → Why not?

問題カード（B日程）　　MP3　アプリ　CD3 79〜82

Helping People in Need

Nowadays in Japan, the number of elderly people is increasing every year. For this reason, barrier-free environments are becoming more and more important. The government is creating them in many places, and by doing so it is making society more convenient for people who need assistance. Barrier-free environments are becoming common in Japan and many other countries around the world.

Your story should begin with this sentence: **One day, Taro and his father were talking in their living room.**

Questions

No. 1   According to the passage, how is the government making society more convenient for people who need assistance?

No. 2   Now, please look at the picture and describe the situation. You have 20 seconds to prepare. Your story should begin with the sentence on the card.
<20 seconds>
Please begin.

Now, Mr. / Ms. ——, please turn over the card and put it down.

No. 3   Some people say that people's manners in public places are getting worse. What do you think about that?

No. 4   Today, computer games are popular with people of all ages. Do you think playing computer games is a waste of time?
Yes.   → Why?
No.   → Why not?

MEMO

MEMO

旺文社の英検®書

☆ 一発合格したいなら「全問＋パス単」！
旺文社が自信を持っておすすめする王道の組み合わせです。

過去問集 ☆ 過去問で出題傾向をしっかりつかむ！
英検®過去6回全問題集 1〜5級
[音声アプリ対応] [音声ダウンロード] [別売CDあり]

単熟語集 ☆ 過去問を徹底分析した「でる順」！
英検®でる順パス単 1〜5級
[音声アプリ対応] [音声ダウンロード]

模試 本番形式の予想問題で総仕上げ！
7日間完成 英検®予想問題ドリル 1〜5級
[CD付] [音声アプリ対応]

参考書 申し込みから面接まで英検のすべてがわかる！
英検®総合対策教本 1〜5級
[CD付]

問題集 大問ごとに一次試験を集中攻略！
DAILY英検®集中ゼミ 1〜5級
[CD付]

二次対策 動画で面接をリアルに体験！
英検®二次試験・面接完全予想問題 1〜3級
[DVD+CD付] [音声アプリ対応]

このほかにも多数のラインナップを揃えております。

旺文社の英検®合格ナビゲーター https://eiken.obunsha.co.jp/
英検合格を目指す方のためのウェブサイト。
試験情報や級別学習法，おすすめの英検書を紹介しています。

※英検®は，公益財団法人 日本英語検定協会の登録商標です。

株式会社 旺文社　〒162-8680　東京都新宿区横寺町55
https://www.obunsha.co.jp/